Essential Elements of

Business Economics

Mark Sutcliffe

Mark Sutcliffe lectures in business economics, international trade and finance, and research methodology at the University of the West of England, Bristol.

He has written and contributed to a number of economics and business text books.

Series adviser: Bob Cudmore BEd, MBA, Head of Management and Professional Studies Division, South Birmingham College

Technical adviser: Bob Glover BEd BA(Econ) Hons, South Birmingham College

Published in association with South Birmingham College
DP Publications Ltd
1994

Acknowledgments

In preparing this book I owe a huge debt of gratitutde to my wife Sheila who not only corrected my errors but dealt with my moods. A special thanks also goes to Martin Sullivan whose helpful comments and suggestions were invaluable. Last but not least a special mention is reserved for John Sloman, without whom my journey into economics would never have begun.

A CIP catalogue reference for this book is available from the British Library

ISBN 1 85805 095 2

Copyright © Mark Sutcliffe, 1994

Typeset by Liz Elwin and KAI

Printed in Great Britain by the Guernsey Press Co. Ltd, Vale, Guernsey

Preface

Aim

The aim of the *Essential Elements* series is to provide course support material covering the main subject areas of HND/C Business Studies and equivalent level courses at a price that students can afford. Students can select titles to suit the requirements of their own particular courses whether BTEC Certificate in Business Administration, Certificate in Marketing, IPS Foundation, Institute of Bankers, Access to Business Studies, Institute of Personnel Management, or other appropriate undergraduate and professional courses.

Many courses now have a modular structure, i.e. individual subjects are taught in a relatively short period of, say, 10 to 12 weeks. The *Essential Elements* series meets the need for material which can be built into the students' study programmes and used for directed self-study. All the texts, therefore, include activities with answers for students' self-assessment, activities for lecturer-assessment, and references to further reading.

The series is a joint venture between DP Publications and South Birmingham College.

How to use the series

All the books in the series are intended to be used as workbooks and provide approximately 70 hours of study material. Each text covers the essential elements of that subject, so that the core of any course at this level is covered, leaving the lecturer to add supplementary material if required. All have the following features:

☐ **In-text activities,** which aim to promote understanding of the principles, and are set at frequent intervals in the text. The solutions add to the student's knowledge, as well as providing an introduction to the next learning point.

☐ **End of chapter exercises**, some of which are intended for self-assessment by the student (these have solutions at the back of the book). Others are suitable for setting by the lecturer and answers or marking guides are provided in the Lecturers' Supplement. These exercises include progress and review questions, multiple choice questions, which test specific knowledge and allow rapid marking, practice questions, and assignments.

☐ **Further reading references** for students who wish to follow up particular topics in more depth.

☐ **Lecturers' Supplement**, which is available free of charge to lecturers adopting the book as a course text. It includes answers or guides to marking to help with student assessment.

Other titles in the series

Available 1994: Financial Accounting, Business Planning and Policy, Business Stattisics, Management Accounting, Marketing, Quantitative Methods.

Available 1995: Business Law, Human Resource Management, Management Information Systems, Operations Management.

Contents

14 *The European union and the business environment*

1 An introduction to business economics

1.1 Introduction

Of all the problems a business might face, those linked to economic issues will be amongst the most important it will have to consider. In this chapter we shall assess how economic factors have a major impact upon the business decision making process.

On completing this chapter you should be able to:

- ❐ identify different levels of economic analysis;
- ❐ outline a range of economic issues facing the business at each of these levels of analysis;
- ❐ explain how economic factors interact with other decision making influences.

1.2 Levels of economic analysis

In economics it is traditional to distinguish between **microeconomic** and **macroeconomic** issues. Microeconomics focuses upon the activities of the individual firm or the individual consumer. Macroeconomics focuses upon issues that face all firms and consumers, in other words macroeconomics is concerned with the economy as a whole.

Although such a division may be suitable in classifying between broad sets of economic problems, on closer inspection we find that a finer distinction is necessary if we are to distinguish between the different levels of problem that a business might face.

As shown in Figure 1.1 we can identify four levels of economic analysis that a business might need to consider.

Figure 1.1 Levels of economic analysis

❏ **The firm**. Economic issues facing the business at this level of analysis will be primarily concerned with problems of production; price setting, costs, revenues and organizational structure. These issues will be considered in Chapters 2–5.

❏ **The market and industry**. Economic issues facing the business at this level analysis will tend to focus upon the implications of the market's structure for business performance; the number and size of firms and the limitations on market expansion. These issues will be considered in Chapters 6–8.

❏ **The national economy**. Economic issues facing the business at this level of analysis are concerned with the problems of overall national economic performance. For example; the level of interest rates, the rate of economic growth, rates of taxation. Such issues will be analysed in Chapters 9–12.

❏ **The international economy**. Economic issues facing the business at this level of analysis will be concerned with problems of international trade; rates of exchange, access into overseas markets, the implications of overseas investment. These issues will be considered in Chapters 13 and 14.

Activity

Classify the following issues into one or more of the levels of analysis identified above:
i) an increase in competition from firms in the Far East.
ii) government tightens legislation concerning restrictive practices policy.
iii) confidence in the future performance of the economy falls.
iv) the European Union refuses to cut its subsidy to support its agricultural sector.

All the issues identified above will influence more than one level of economic analysis. Both (i) and (iv) will have international as well as market or industry implications for business. In (ii) a tighter restrictive practices policy will have a major impact upon the firm and industry level of analysis. In (iii) a fall in business confidence will have its most significant impact upon the performance of the national economy as a whole.

1.3 Other determinants in decision making – a PEST analysis

Faced with such distinct levels of analysis how does management attempt to construct a business strategy? One common approach employed by business is to conduct a PEST analysis. A PEST analysis involves considering what political, economic, social and technological factors will influence a business over a given period of time. A business will attempt in each case to identify in what manner the various factors might be both an opportunity and or a threat to its future plans.

An example of a PEST analysis is shown below. This analysis refers to the defence sector in the South West of England during 1991 and illustrates the various considerations defence contractors have had to take into account when deciding upon their business strategy.

	Strengths	Weaknesses
Political	Industry is a powerful lobby group – ability to influence government	End of the Cold War Cuts in defence spending Lack of long-term government action
Economic	Skilled labour force Specialist service	Economic specialism creates dependency Vulnerable to world economic activity Impact upon regional economy of defence cutbacks such as regional unemployment Costs of restructuring Direction of restructuring, i.e. what markets to locate in
Social	Pro-active management culture Union committment to business	
Technological	High technology base	Need for constant innovation R & D cost

Activity

Conduct your own PEST analysis on a local industry or consider a large national industry such as car production.

In your analysis, as well as considering domestic influences, you must also focus upon international factors that might influence the businesses performance.

Summary

In the following chapters we will consider in more detail the economic considerations that the business must take into account when formulating its business strategy. However, it must be recognised that economic considerations represent only one set of factors that business needs to consider.

Further reading

Sloman J, *Economics*, Harvester Wheatsheaf, 1994, Chapter 1.

Sloman J and Sutcliffe M, *Economics Workbook*, Harvester Wheatsheaf, 1994, Chapter 1.

Progress questions

1. Macroeconomics is the study of individual consumer behaviour. True ☐ False ☐

2. There are four levels of economic analysis, these are:

   (i) .... (ii) .... (iii)............................ (iv)............................

3. A PEST analysis is: ....

Review questions

4. Why are different levels of economic analysis important when considering the formulation of a businesses economic strategy? (Section 1.2)

5. What factors other than economics might influence the decision making process of business? Give examples showing the impact of such factors. (Section 1.3)

Multiple choice questions

6. Which of the following is **not** a microeconomic issue:
    (a) a shortage in the supply of labour to a local car manufacturer.
    (b) an increase in competition facing a firm.
    (c) a rise in company taxation.
    (d) a fall in an industries profits due to rising raw material costs.

7. Which of the following is **not** a macroeconomic issue:
    (a) the rate of economic growth falls.
    (b) the banking sector cuts the size of its labour force.
    (c) unemployment rises.
    (d) the competitiveness of the UK's export sector rises.

Practice questions

8. Why have international economic considerations, in recent years, become more important in shaping business strategy?

Assignment

Select a local business near to where you live. Consider what factors will influence its economic performance and attempt to identify those factors which might shape its business strategy. If possible you might attempt to arrange an interview with one of the businesses managers to gain information.

Present your findings as a report highlighting the political, economic, social and technological factors that are relevant to your selected business.

2 Resource allocation

2.1 Introduction

In this chapter we will consider the problems that face all societies in deciding how to allocate its scarce resources between many competing uses and the role of business in this task.

On completing this chapter you should be able to:

❑ define the term scarcity;

❑ define and illustrate the concept of opportunity cost;

❑ distinguish between alternative economic systems;

❑ outline the advantages and disadvantages of each type of economic system;

❑ assess the arguments both for and against privatisation.

2.2 The problem of scarcity

All economic systems face the problem of **scarcity**. What differs between them is how they attempt to resolve this problem. Scarcity, in an economic sense, is due to the fact that individuals have unlimited wants. That is, they want more consumer durables, more holidays, a second home etc. However, the means of fulfilling such wants is limited by the availability of economic resources. We must therefore make choices between the competing goods and services that such resources can be used to produce.

Economic resources are the basic inputs used in the production of goods and services. They are frequently called **factors of production** and are classified as:

❑ **Land.** There is only a fixed supply of land and hence a limited supply of raw materials within the land.

❑ **Labour.** Human resources such as labour are limited both in number and in the skills that labour holds.

❑ **Capital.** Capital refers to the number of factories, machines, etc., that are used in the productive process.

❑ **Enterprise.** Enterprise is the process whereby land, labour and capital are brought together, combined and organized to produce output. Such entrepreneurial ability may be classified as a scarce resource.

Activity

Capital as a resource is created by society. The process of creating capital is known as investment. Is it in any way more important than the other factors of production?

Improvements in the stock of capital enables us to use scarce resources more efficiently, improving productivity by producing more output from a given quantity of input. In this respect capital is more important than the other factors of production.

2.3 *The production possibility curve and opportunity cost*

Given that not all the wants of society can be met, one good is consumed or produced at the cost of another good. This is known as the **opportunity cost.** For example the opportunity cost to the individual of purchasing a new compact disc might be that they are unable to purchase some essential course texts for their studies. This same principle can be applied to the economy as a whole not just the individual, more cars may mean less motorbikes; or, in relation to government spending, more on health care may mean less on education. In all these cases choices are being made concerning the allocation of scarce resources.

The principle of opportunity cost and choice can be illustrated using a simple diagram known as the **production possibility curve.** Assume that in a simple economy only two goods are produced, compact disc players and jeans. To produce more of one will involve producing less of the other. If we assume that all resources are efficiently used, then we can derive a curve showing the maximum levels of output of these goods given the level of resources available and the current state of technology. In figure 2.1, X represents a point where we produce 1,000 CD players or 3,000 jeans. If we shift production to point Y, this means that the opportunity cost of producing one thousand more CD players is the loss of two thousand pairs of jeans.

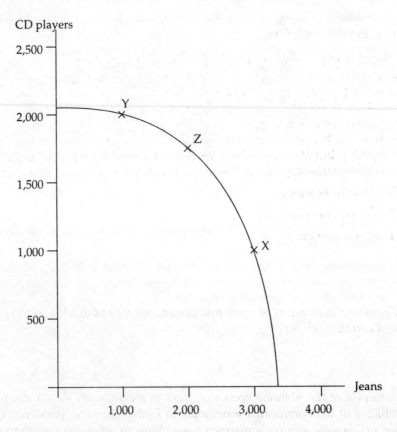

Figure 2.1 A production possibility curve

Activity

Given the production possibility curve above, answer the following:

(i) What is the opportunity cost of moving from point Y to point Z?

(ii) Explain why the curve is bowed outward from the origin and is not simply a straight line?

(iii) What is likely to happen to the production possibility curve over time?

The opportunity cost of moving from Y to Z is loss of 250 CDs in order to produce an additional 1,000 pairs of jeans. The bowed nature of the curve reflects increasing opportunity costs. This occurs due to the fact that producing more of one unit takes a growing amount of resource used in producing the other unit. In a given society not all resources will be suited to produce CD players; the less suited such resources are the less productive they become, the more resource will be needed to produce a given quantity of output. Hence the bowed nature of the curve reflects this phenomena. Over time the production possibility curve will shift to the right, more CD players and more jeans may be produced. There are two reasons you might identify to explain this. The first is that the available level of resources has grown. For example the population has expanded. And second, the level of technology has advanced thus enabling available resources to be more effectively used. Thus, the production process has experienced rising productivity, and more output can now be generated per unit of input.

2.4 Classifying economic systems

How do societies set about making choices between the immense number of goods and services offered? What or who determines how such goods and services are to be produced, and subsequently how they are to be allocated amongst the various members of society? Different societies have found different answers to these questions and the problem of resource allocation. We can identify three types of economic system. Such systems are distinguished from one another, not only on the basis of ownership but also concerning the level of government involvement in the process of economic decision-making. The three broad categories of economic system are the:

❒ **planned economy**

❒ **free market economy**

❒ **mixed economy**

Activity

Given the three types of economic system can you identify a country or countries to illustrate each type?

Examples of the planned economy, have in recent years all but disappeared with the collapse of the communist economies in Eastern Europe. However, China and Cuba are still largely run on a planned basis. Most of what are referred to as free market economies are in reality mixed economies, that is they all involve some government intervention in the running of economic affairs. Where they differ is in the mix of market forces and government intervention. The UK, USA and Hong Kong for example are more free market orientated than for example, France and Sweden, who are far more actively interventionist when allocating societies scarce resources.

2.5 The planned economy

The planned economy has been largely associated with the socialist/communist economic system. However, many variations concerning how the economy might be planned can be identified, from the wholesale ownership of industry to the setting of national production targets. Within this type of economic system the state attempts to plan, control and influence the allocation of society's resources, for example:

❏ between present consumption and future investment;

❏ between industries and firms;

❏ between consumers such that output is distributed on criteria of need or possibly on how much each individual produces.

The advantages of a planned economy are that:

❏ resources can be more fairly distributed amongst the population;

❏ the state can plan for the future;

❏ problems like unemployment and inflation can be controlled.

Activity

What problems might a planned economy experience?

We might identify the following:

❏ the task of planning is highly complex and inefficient due to poor information concerning what resources are available and in what quantities;

❏ prices set by the state do not reflect the relative scarcity of goods and services;

❏ without worker and producer incentives such as profits and wage bonuses, production is inefficient suffering from both low productivity and quality;

❏ there is limited consumer choice.

2.6 The free market economy

The free market economy is associated with the capitalist economic system. Within such an economy the operation of the **price mechanism** determines the level of supply and demand and the subsequent allocation of resources between competing goods and services.

Prices act as:

❏ a reflection of a goods or services scarcity;

❏ a source of information for buyers and sellers;

❏ an incentive to produce or consume.

The advantages of the free market are that:

❑ the market mechanism operates automatically and responds quickly to changes in demand and supply;

❑ competition leads to greater efficiency;

❑ there is freedom of consumer choice.

The disadvantages of the free market are that:

❑ competition between firms is limited due to large firms having market power and the ability to set rather than respond to prices;

❑ it will fail to produce certain goods and services known as **public goods**, because it is unprofitable or impractical to do so;

❑ it will under-provide certain goods and services which are of benefit to society as a whole. These are known as **merit goods**;

❑ the prices of goods and services do not take account of the external costs of production such as pollution. This is known as an **externality**;

❑ output is distributed on the ability to pay and not need;

❑ markets tend to be constantly fluctuating, this makes it difficult to plan for the future.

Activity

Classify the list of goods and services below into merit goods and public goods. Consider how far in each case the market is or is not capable of providing such goods and services.

A lighthouse	National Defence	Meals on wheels
Public housing	Education	Health

A lighthouse and national defence are examples of public goods. The market would not provide these goods as it would be unable to charge a price to all users/consumers. It would be both unprofitable and impractical to attempt to do so. They suffer from what is known as the **free rider** problem. The other items are merit goods. If left to the individuals ability to pay, these services would not be produced in sufficient quantities. This would be undesirable for a society which benefits from a well educated, healthy and housed population.

2.7 The mixed economy

Most, if not all, economies in the world are of the mixed type. The mixed economy is an attempt to combine the efficiency of the free market and price mechanism with the equity and stability of the planned economy. State intervention can range from:

❑ the direct provision of goods and service, such as via the nationalised industries or through the welfare state, for example health care and education.

❑ the use of economic policy to manage the economy;

❑ the use of legislative powers to control economic behaviour, such as the Monopolies and Mergers Commission (MMC) to regulate big business.

Activity

One way in which the state might intervene in the economy is to set prices. Such prices might be above or below what the free market price would be. Explain why the state might wish prices to be at a different level to that determined by the market?

By fixing prices the state is attempting to alter the distribution of income. By fixing a price above equilibrium, known as a **price floor** (prices will not fall below it), the incomes of suppliers is protected. An example of this is the Common Agricultural Policy (CAP); high food prices protect and maintain the incomes of farmers. The setting of a **price ceiling** (prices will not rise above it), that is a price below equilibrium, may be used to protect the interest of consumers who would be excluded from the market if prices were any higher. Fair rent policies regulating the level of rent in the private sector would be one way of ensuring fairer access to housing for a larger share of the population.

In both of the above instances the setting of minimum and maximum prices is not without implications. In order to maintain the CAP the European Union is forced to buy the surplus production the system of price subsidy creates. In the past this has led to huge mountains of food which in many cases were put into storage or destroyed. In order to keep rents down in the private housing market, the state was forced to provide its own housing as many landlords withdrew their houses from the market place, attempting to find a more profitable alternative use. Without such additional provision less houses would have been available to rent and homelessness might have risen. This suggests that intervention might be costly.

2.8 Privatisation

In recent years many economies, the UK in particular, have seen a significant change in the mix between free markets and state intervention in the running of economic affairs. The most significant of these changes has been through the policy of **privatisation**. The implementation of this policy has been as dramatic as the shift towards nationalisation in 1945. The most significant form of privatisation has involved the selling of state-owned industries to the general public. In the UK the privatisation programme began in earnest from 1983 when the government announced that the major public utilities such as telecommunications, gas, water and electricity were to be sold. The arguments advanced to support this programme were that:

☐ industries were to be exposed to market forces, making them more efficient and responsive to the wishes of the consumer;

☐ such business would be free from the manipulation of government;

☐ privatised industries would no longer be a burden on the tax payer, who had in many cases provided grants and subsidies so that they could remain in business;

☐ it would encourage wider share ownership;

☐ it helped provide finance for government to embark on alternative policies.

Activity

Privatisation has not been without its critics. What arguments might we advance against the privatisation of state owned industry?

The following criticisms of privatisation have been raised:

❐ it was difficult to introduce significant competition into a market where you have a **natural monopoly**, that is a market where only one firm can effectively provide supply;

❐ the new privatised monopolies would have significant market power and as such would be very difficult to control;

❐ the selling of such industries means that any profits made in the future would not go to the state, the financial gain from privatisation is largely short term;

❐ criteria used to assess the performance of privatised industries such as profit and productivity should not imply that nationalised industries did less well. Industries were frequently nationalised because they were not profitable, their aim was however to maintain employment. Therefore, comparing a business before and after privatisation needs to consider these differing goals when assessing notions of success.

2.9   Summary

In this chapter we have considered how scarce resources can be allocated between competing uses. We have identified three alternative economic systems and analysed the advantages and disadvantages that each system has to offer. No one system is perfect and frequently the mix between the market and the state is as much to do with the political commitments of a country as it is to do with sound economics. It should be clear from our analysis that the role of business organisations in each type of system will vary, from total control by the state, to free enterprise, to government regulation.

Further reading

Sloman J, *Economics*, Harvester Wheatsheaf, 1994, Chapter 1.

Sloman J and Sutcliffe M, *Economics Workbook*, Harvester Wheatsheaf, 1994, Chapter 1.

Livesey F, *A Textbook of Economics*, Longman, 1989, Chapters 2 and 3.

Progress questions

1.   All economic systems face the economic problem of: ....

2.   The four factors of production are: ....

3.   The opportunity cost of a good is: ....

4.   The three main categories of economic system are: ....

5. A planned economy is one where consumers are given a wide choice of goods.

   True ☐ False ☐

6. A free market economy will help businesses to plan long term. True ☐ False ☐

7. An externality is: ....

8. Explain the difference between a public and a merit good: ....

   ....

9. Give three examples of state intervention in a mixed economy: ....

   ....

10. Privatisation means: ....

Review questions

11. Explain how the production possibility curve illustrates the concept of opportunity cost. (Section 2.3)

12. What are the principle differences between a planned economy and a free market economy? (Section 2.5 and 2.6)

13. Do the disadvantages of having a free market outweigh the advantages? (Section 2.6)

14. What does a mixed economy hope to achieve? (Section 2.7)

15. Distinguish between the short run gains of privatisation and the long run losses. (Section 2.8)

Multiple choice questions

16. If the production possibility curve shifts outward from the origin this might reflect:
    (a) a growing abundance of resources.
    (b) a rise in productivity.
    (c) the development of new technology.
    (d) all of the above.

17. Which of the following is **not** true of the free market economic system:
    (a) merit goods and public goods will be under produced.
    (b) market fluctuations create uncertainty.
    (c) competition ensures efficiency.
    (d) there will be limited consumer choice.

18. Which of the following industries has **not** been privatised:
    (a) British Telecom
    (b) British Gas
    (c) The Royal Mail
    (d) British Rail

Practice questions

19. Why do all economic systems face the problem of scarcity?

20. Why might we argue that a mixed economy is superior to both the free market and the planned economy?

21. Make a case both for and against privatisation.

Assignment

Conduct an investigation into either the privatisation of electricity or rail. Your investigation should focus upon the structure of the industry following privatisation and how this is intended to increase competition. Consider whether it will be successful in this respect.

3 Business organisations

3.1 Introduction

In the previous chapter we considered the issues of resource allocation, in this chapter and the next two we will consider how individual enterprises set about making production and output decisions.

On completing this chapter you should be able to:

- distinguish between different types of business organizations;
- assess the advantages and disadvantages of alternative organizational structures;
- identify a range of objectives that business might pursue;
- outline a variety of business growth strategy;
- define and identify economies of scale;
- describe the main problems presented by big business;
- outline the main goals of UK and European competition policy.

3.2 Types of business organisation

The range and nature of decisions that an individual firm may take concerning production will not only depend upon the structure of the market (dealt with in Chapter 6) but will also be influenced by the size of the individual business organization. The following types of business organization can be identified:

- **The sole proprietor/trader**. This business is owned by just one person. It tends to be small, with few if any employees. Such businesses are easy to set up and only require limited capital investment. They tend to be very responsive to changing market conditions. However, they have only a limited scope for expansion depending upon the owners own resources or personal borrowing, and the owner is personally liable for any losses that the business might make.

- **The partnership**. This is where two but no more than 20 people own the business. With more owners, there is more scope for expansion. More finance can be raised and the partners can each specialise in different aspects of the business. Partners, have unlimited liability. Thus where large amounts of capital are required the risk of business failure can be very high for the individual partner's.

- **Companies**. A company, or joint stock company to give it its full title, is legally separate from its owners. Any debts are its debts, not the owners. The owners have limited liability. This means that if the company goes bankrupt the owners only lose the amount of money they have invested in the company. There are two types of companies. **Public limited companies** are called so because they can offer new shares publicly. They are often quoted on the Stock Exchange. The price of these shares is determined by demand and supply. The **private limited company** cannot offer its shares publicly. Shares have to be sold privately. This makes it more difficult for private limited companies to raise finance and consequently they tend to be smaller then public companies and run as family businesses. They are however, easier to set up than public companies.

❑ **Public corporations**. These are state-owned enterprises such as the BBC, the Bank of England and the nationalised industries (British Rail, the Post Office etc). They have a legal identity separate from the government. However, the board, appointed to run the corporation by the relevant government minister, must act within various terms of reference laid down by statute.

❑ **Consortia of firms**. It is common, especially in civil engineering projects that involve very high risks, for many firms to work together as a consortium. The Channel Tunnel and Thames Barrier are examples of this form of business organization. Within the consortia one firm may act as the managing contractor, while the other members may provide specialist services. Alternatively management may be equally shared.

Activity

In table 3.1 below is a breakdown by the size of business of the construction industry in 1991. What does it tell us about this industry and the importance of business size?

Size of firm	Number	%	Work done (£ million)	%	Employment (Thousands)	%
1	103,169	(49.7)	809.3	(8.7)	94.5	(11.0)
2–3	70,452	(34.0)	883.5	(9.5)	147.5	(17.0)
4–7	21,664	(10.4)	754.5	(8.2)	91.9	(10.5)
8–13	4,981	(2.4)	435.8	(4.7)	49.8	(5.7)
14–24	3,429	(1.6)	615.8	(6.7)	61.0	(7.0)
25–114	3,040	(1.5)	1748.5	(19.0)	144.5	(16.7)
115–1,199	626	(0.3)	2621.2	(28.4)	176.5	(20.4)
1,200 and over	39	(0.02)	1369.2	(14.8)	100.6	(11.6)
All firms	207,400	(100.0)	9237.6	(100.0)	866.6	(100.0)

Table 3.1 The construction industry 1991

We can see from the data that there is a very large small firm sector in the construction industry. Over 83% of all business have no more than three employees. However, such firms only account for 28% of employment and a mere 18.2% of the value of the work done. Conversely large firms, 1,200 employees and over, accounted for only 0.02% of all firms yet employed 11% of total construction labour and earned 14.8% of the total value of construction output.

3.3 Business organizations and their internal structure

The internal operating structures of many businesses is largely dictated by there size. Small firms tend to be centrally managed and decision making taken by a clear managerial hierarchy. This internal structure is often referred to as a **U-form organiz-ational structure**. When firms expand spans of control widen and problems may occur in maintaining effective managerial control. Firms may attempt to solve this problem by reorganizing their business structure. The formation of separate operating companies which control their own day to day decision making will help reduce bureaucracy and improve the general level of business efficiency. This internal structure is often referred to as a **M-form organizational structure**. In this case senior managers focus upon the aims and strategy of the business organization and not its daily administration.

U form management structure

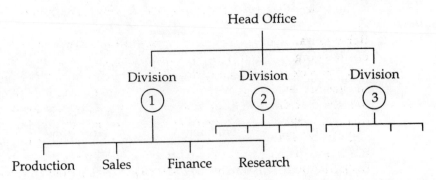

M form management structure

Figure 3.1 U form and M form management structures

Activity

What impact might we anticipate new micro-technology could have on the future internal organization of the firm?

The establishment of computerised networked systems has helped to improve the flow of information within the firm. Managers are now able to exercise a greater span of control. The implications of this might be that (a) fewer managers are required within the business organization, and (b) there will be a significant reduction in communication costs. A return to U form organizational structures might be possible, however unlikely given the flexibility required of business in a modern market economy. Hence a more efficient future use of the M form business organization, with an increasing emphasis on global operations seems more certain.

3.4   Aims of business organizations

Traditional economic theory assumes that the principal aim of a business organization is one of **profit maximisation**. Although firms may aim for other objectives, such as improved working conditions or better salaries, such objectives are of only secondary importance. This theory of the firm was largely formulated at a time when the owner of the firm was also the manager. There was a single interest. However, with the growth in big business and the expansion of the joint stock company, there arose a division between ownership and control, that is management. The owners were no longer the managers. The objective(s) of the business organization became less easy to identify as there was not one but many business interests. Profit maximisation, rather than a single goal of the business, was now seen to act as a simple constraint on other business objectives. So long as shareholders were satisfied with their share dividends the manager was free to pursue a whole range of alternative goals. Such alternative goals might include:

☐ **sales revenue maximisation** – sales are frequently used as a means of bonus payments, such that salaries, power and prestige within the organisation may well depend upon the ability to sell;

☐ **growth maximisation** is a more long-term aim. A large firm generates certain managerial advantages, such as expanding promotion prospects, greater power, and the satisfaction of being with a growing organization.

Behavioural theories of the firm present an alternative approach to understanding the business organization. These theories suggests that an organisations aims are varied and complex and frequently do not involve maximising anything merely achieving a satisfactory level, such as a satisfactory level of sales or level of output. The reasons for this are that different departments within the firm are likely to have conflicting or divergent interests and targets and these are only resolved through compromise and negotiation. For example the sales department might wish to maximise sales, whereas the finance department might wish to minimise costs. A common interest may only be realised if both departments negotiate a jointly acceptable alternative.

Activity

What problems might economists have in attempting to predict the actions of firms if they behave as behavioural theories suggest?

By focusing upon the internal decision making process behavioural theories suggest that the use of a simple model to explain the actions and policies of a manager is unrealistic. Actions may well be subject to regular change and revision. Such actions and policies may, in many cases, be inherently inconsistent from one time period to the next as the influence of departments within the business organization and even the managers themselves change.

3.5 Business organizations and alternative growth strategy

As a consequence of the dynamic competitive process of business, many businesses are forced to expand to remain in the market place. Failure to do so may allow rival firms who do expand to secure a greater share of the market and its profits. Not only in this case is the expansion of business important for its own survival, in many respects it is important for the health of the economy as a whole. Growing business might contribute to:

❑ higher levels of gross investment;

❑ economies of scale (see section 3.6)

❑ technological improvements through the utilization of capital;

❑ higher productivity growth;

❑ improved managerial quality.

Given the importance of a growing business to its owners, managers and the economy as a whole, how might such growth be achieved? Business growth can be classified as coming from either **internal expansion** or **merger**. Internal expansion is whereby the firm either through the use of profits, borrowing or share issue expands its own business operations. Growth by merger in contrast, is expansion gained from the purchase of or merging with an existing business.

Once the business has made the decision to grow and decided whether such growth should be internal or acquired from the purchase of an existing firm, it might pursue a range of different growth strategy. It might attempt to:

❑ **diversify** its business operations. Diversification will allow the firm to spread its risks and hence reduce the uncertainty it faces. It may also be that the main industry within which the business operates constrains its growth, for example the market may be saturated with competition, hence diversification offers a more profitable way to use new investment funds

❑ pursue a strategy of **vertical integration**. Such a strategy will give the business greater security, either through **forward** integration and control of its distribution and retail network, or **backward** integration and control of its supply chain. Such a strategy will also tend to improve efficiency as the business internalises certain transaction costs, and at the same time it will tend to increase the businesses level of market power.

❑ embark upon extensive **research and development** and **product** and **process innovation**. Such a strategy is based upon a long term view, aiming to secure a greater share of the market. New products will yield high future returns and new processes will contribute to reduced costs.

Activity

Why do businesses merge? The figures below in table 3.2 show the main reasons given for merger activity in the European Union. What can we deduce from them?

Mergers and majority acquisitions

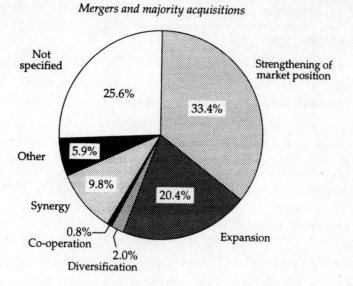

Table 3.2 Merger motives in the European Union 1990

There are many motives why firms might merge the most important factor identified for European merger activity is the desire to strengthen the businesses market position. This is followed by the business seeking to expand, using the merger as a form of growth strategy. The use of merger to diversify the businesses operations appears less common.

3.6 Business organizations and economies and diseconomies of scale

As a business expands the scale of its production (output) will increase, this in turn will influence the businesses production costs. If an increase in output results in lower unit costs we call this **economies of scale**. If an increase in output results in higher unit costs we call this **diseconomies of scale**. Economies and diseconomies of scale can be classified as **internal** and **external** to the firm.

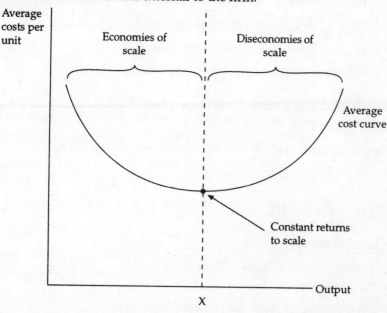

Figure 3.2 Economies and diseconomies of scale

19

Internal economies of scale occur where firms make more effective use of their resources, hence lowering costs and improving productivity. Such internal economies of scale can include:

☐ extending the use of the division of labour and employing more specialist workers;

☐ financial economies such as attracting favourable rates of interest on finance, and cheaper inputs through bulk purchasing;

☐ machinery being used to its full capacity;

☐ the use of production waste to create sellable by-products.

External economies of scale occur from the expansion of the industry as a whole and may be gained by all firms whether they change there size of production or not. These may include:

☐ the creation of a large skilled labour force;

☐ the formation of industrial clusters where related firms in an industry concentrate, such as component suppliers and machinery manufacturers.

Internal diseconomies of scale occur when the firm becomes of such a size as to create inefficiency and push costs up. Such diseconomies might include:

☐ management experiencing problems in co-ordinating the activities of the business as lines of communication become longer;

☐ industrial relations become more impersonal and worker motivation falls;

☐ rising costs caused by the increased use of resources that are in short supply.

External diseconomies of scale may come about as a consequence of industry locating in one particular area, this might have an impact on local infrastructure such as housing and transport, fuelling demands for higher wages and increasing the costs of distribution.

In the long run businesses may attempt to remedy many diseconomics of scale (internal and external) by:

☐ shifting location;

☐ re-organizing the management structure of the firm;

☐ introduce new technology into the productive process.

Activity

What general factors will influence where a business locates?

We might identify three classes of location factor: market, costs and personal. Market factors might include:

☐ location to main market;

☐ location to competitors;

☐ the size of the market;

☐ the competitiveness of the industry in its location.

Cost factors might include:

- ❏ the cost of land;
- ❏ the cost of expanding on an existing site;
- ❏ the offering of regional assistance such as government regional grants;
- ❏ costs of transportation;
- ❏ the availability of labour.

Personal factors might include a wish to improve the work environment, such as moving from an inner city site to a location in the country.

3.7 Big business and the public interest

We have identified that large business might bring with them certain inherent economic advantages such as economies of scale. This may well mean for the consumer that a lower price is paid for the product than if it was produced in a market structure where firms were of a smaller scale. However, large firms may in fact in many instances operate against the public interest. Large firms may:

- ❏ erect certain **barriers to entry**, restricting the entry of new firms into the market, thereby reducing competitive pressures;
- ❏ charge a higher price and produce a lower level of output than in markets where a greater number of smaller businesses might operate;
- ❏ have higher costs due to a lack of competition, this is known as **X-inefficiency**;
- ❏ suffer from inertia and fail to innovate and exploit market opportunities.

Activity

If large firms were capable of erecting barriers to entry what form might they take?

There are many different types of barrier to entry that large firms might adopt. These could include economies of scale; advertising; the ownership of key factors of production; control over retail outlets; the threat of merger; legal protection such as patents and the use of aggressive tactics such as running at a loss to drive new entrants out of the market.

3.8 Controlling big business: Competition Policy in the UK and Europe

Given that large firms have some degree of market power, and that such power might be used against the public interest, it has become a major concern of government to ensure that such firms do not abuse there position. **Competition Policy** in the UK and Europe focuses upon three area:

- ❏ monopoly policy;
- ❏ merger policy;
- ❏ restrictive practices policy.

Monopoly policy is concerned with whether the actions of a business is in the public interest, most significant of which would be its setting of price. **Merger policy** aims to monitor merger activity and assess whether the new merged firm would be in the public interest. If not then such a merger would be blocked. **Restrictive practices**

policy assesses whether collusive agreements between firms, such as output restrictions or price agreements are operating against the public interest.

The **Monopolies and Merger Commission (MMC)** which was set up in 1948, and the **Office of Fair Trading (OFT)** set up in 1973, are the principle agencies that deal with competition policy in the UK. Since 1948 legislation to deal with anti-competitive practices has been reformulated and added to progressively. Has it proved successful?

The difficulty in assessing the success of such policy is the vague definition given to the concept of public interest. Although clearer now, prior to 1973 it was very much a discretionary decision made by the investigating panel. Today the public interest is assessed against the criteria of **effective competition**, that is sufficient competition in order to ensure lower costs and the interests of the consumer being met in respect to other factors such as quality and service.

Whether restrictive practice policy has been successful forces us to make a distinction between agreements between firms that are open and formal and those that are hidden or tacit. Formal collusion has been virtually eradicated. However, the extent of hidden collusion is difficult to assess.

Monopoly and merger policy has been accused of being inconsistent and on the whole ineffective. Of 3000 mergers since 1965 only 100 have been referred to the MMC. The MMC has stopped in total 60 proposed mergers. As a proportion of all mergers which have fallen within it bounds to investigate, that is holding a market share of 25% or acquiring assets valued at £30m or more, this accounts for no more than 2% of the total.

EU competition policy is seen as a vital component in establishing an integrated European market. In many cases EU legislation is far stricter than legislation in the UK. Equally the powers of the competition department to investigate unfair market practices and enforce such measures are significantly greater than those of the MMC. The Director General of the competition department can raid companies, seize documents, levy fines of up to 10% of turnover and even bloc mergers over 5bn ECU.

Activity

Investigations by the MMC in the UK and the Director General in Europe, are frequently reported in the quality press. Find a recent case, either in the UK or Europe, and prepare a report on the issues it raised and the outcome of the investigation.

Summary

In this chapter we have considered the various organizational structures of business and how such businesses might set about growing. We have also considered the advantages and disadvantages that large firms can produce and the problems that government faces in defending the public interest. This chapter helps to prepare the foundations for the following chapters which consider how businesses operate in a dynamic economic environment.

Further reading

Sloman J, *Economics*, Harvester Wheatsheaf, 1994, Chapter 5 Section 5.2 and Chapter 8 (for advanced students only).

Sloman J and Sutcliffe M, *Economics Workbook*, Harvester Wheatsheaf, 1994, Chapter 5 questions 17–20.

Dunnet A, *Understanding the Market* Longman, 1992, Chapter 8 sections 8.1 and 8.2.

Progress questions

1. Give three differences between a sole trader and a public limited company ....
....

2. A U-form managerial structure enables management to operate a greater span of control.

   True ☐ False ☐

3. List three maximisation aims of business ....
....

4. Behavioural theories of the firm mean that business behaviour is less predictable.

   True ☐ False ☐

5. Give five reasons why competition and business growth is desirable for the economy as a whole.

   ....

6. Distinguish between internal expansion and growth by merger ....
....

7. Identify three growth strategy ....
....

8. Economies of scale mean greater efficiency.   True ☐ False ☐

9. Diseconomies of scale are only a problem in the long run.   True ☐ False ☐

10. Give four reasons why big business may operate against the public interest ....
....

Review questions

11. How is the internal operating structure of a business linked to its size? (Section 3.3)

12. What are the main differences between the traditional economic theory of the businesses aim and that of the behaviouralist theory. (Section 3.4)

13. Assess the advantages and disadvantages of alternative business growth strategy. (Section 3.5)

14. Distinguish between internal and external economies of scale and offer examples. (Section 3.6)

15. Can competition policy effectively control the actions of big business? (Section 3.8)

Multiple choice questions

16. Which of the following is not an internal economy of scale:
    (a) greater specialisation in the process of production.
    (b) the size of the industrial labour force increases.
    (c) the business attracts a more favourable rate of interest on finance.
    (d) machines are more efficiently run with higher levels of production.

17. Which of the following is **not** a barrier to entry? Is it:
    (a) advertising.
    (b) economies of scale.
    (c) low business start-up costs.
    (d) the threat of merger.

18. Cases of restrictive practices are, in the UK, investigated by:
    (a) The Monopolies and Mergers Commission.
    (b) The Office of Fair Trading.
    (c) The Department of Trade and Industry.
    (d) the competition department in the European Union.

Practice questions

19. What types of business organisation might we identify? What links will the size of the business organisation have with its internal operating structure?

20. What factors might influence the type of growth strategy adopted by a business?

21. How might big business operate against the public interest? What can competition policy do to control such actions?

Assignment

Taking a well-known UK business, prepare a company profile. You should attempt to gather information on your chosen business so as to assess its economic performance since 1979. Consider how it has grown and in what manner its growth has been achieved. Other factors you might consider in your analysis are profits, sales, share value, capital investment, number of employees and overseas operations.

4 Business organisations and production

4.1 Introduction

Whatever the divergent aims of managers might be they must all make a series of crucial decisions concerning the production of goods or services. The decision to produce depends upon a range of considerations determined by the market within which the organisation operates, as well as overall managerial objectives. Such decisions might focus upon:

❑ whether the demand for the good/service is growing, constant or declining;

❑ the price to be charged;

❑ the impact on costs and revenue of selecting alternative levels of output.

On completing this chapter you should be able to:

❑ describe what is meant by the terms demand and supply and identify those factors that influence their level;

❑ construct a diagram of a simple market;

❑ define and use the concept of elasticity.

4.2 The production decision: demand

In this section and the next we will construct a simple market, first we will focus on demand and then supply.

The demand for a good is represented by a simple inverse relationship. As the price of a good falls, the quantity demanded increases. Alternatively, a rise in price causes the quantity demanded to fall. This relationship can be explained by considering either (i), the impact that the change in price has upon consumer income; a price fall means that consumer income has risen and more can now be consumed. Or (ii), by noting that the cheaper the product is, the more attractive it becomes. Rational consumers will substitute the cheaper for the more expensive alternative that they might already consume. If we derive an individual demand curve as shown in figure 4.1a, we are illustrating how much the consumer is willing to purchase at any price. The market demand curve is simply the summation of all the individual consumer demand curves.

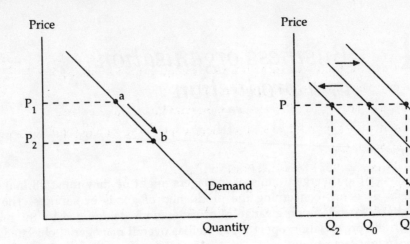

Figure 4.1a An individual demand curve   Figure 4.1b Shifts in demand

Price is not the only determinant of demand. Other factors which might influence the total quantity demanded are:

☐ consumer tastes;

☐ the number and price of **substitute goods**, for example butter and margarine;

☐ the number and price of **complementary goods**, for example frozen food and freezers;

☐ the level of consumer income;

☐ fashion and advertising;

☐ expectations, for example of future price changes or supply shortages.

We may distinguish between the influence of price and the other factors on demand by noting that changes in price will involve movements **along** the curve, whereas changes in the other determinants cause the demand curve to **shift**. In figure 4.1b a rightward shift of the demand curve signifies a rising level of demand, whereas a leftward shift a falling level of demand.

Traditional consumer theory assumes that the individual consumer takes all the above conditions into consideration when making a purchasing decision. The consumer is assumed to be perfectly informed about the quality of the products on offer; the price and availability of substitutes and complements; and will use this information to maximise their satisfaction (utility).

More modern approaches to consumer theory suggest that factors other than price, such as, quality, reliability, design, performance and after-sales service, play a significant part in determining consumer decisions. If price is not the only thing that consumers are interested in, managers must think carefully about how they market and present their goods and services.

Activity

How will the following influence the demand curve for video games?

(a) the price of video game players fall?

(b) an advertising war breaks out between video game rivals?

(c) a medical report suggests that video games may damage children's health?

(d) summer time?

(e) the chancellor lowers tax in the budget?

(f) a new board game enters the market?

(g) video games become more expensive?

(a) the curve will shift right, as video games and video game players are complementary. (b) the curve will shift right if the advertising campaign is a success! (c) the curve will shift left. (d) the curve will shift left as during summertime the better weather enables people to pursue a wider range of leisure activities. (e) the curve will shift right as real income rises. (f) the curve will shift left as a new substitute becomes available. (g) there will be a movement up and along the demand curve, no shift.

4.3   The production decision: supply

The relationship between price and quantity and the decision to supply is a direct relationship. That is the higher the price of a good, the greater the wish of suppliers to supply to the market. It may mean that more profit is achieved in doing so. Conversely, the lower the price, the less incentive suppliers have to supply. When we derive a supply curve, as in figure 4.2a, we are showing how much producers are prepared to supply at all market prices.

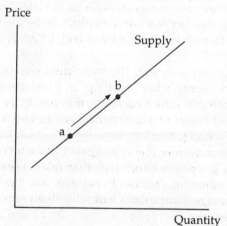
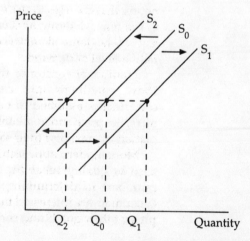

Figure 4.2a An individual supply curve

Figure 4.2b Shifts in supply

Price is not the only determinant of supply. Other factors which might influence the quantity supplied include:

❑ the costs of production, including the application of a particular type of technology;

❑ the aims of producers. Profit maximisers will reach different supply decisions to sales maximisers;

❏ prices of other products. More profitable alternative products may cause a shift in production;

❏ expectations of future price changes. Producers may reduce current supply by stock-piling goods if a price rise is expected in the future.

As with demand we may distinguish between changes in price, which will involve a movement along the supply curve, and changes in the other factors of supply which will cause the supply curve to shift. A rightward shift in the supply curve signifies a supply increase, whereas a leftward shift a supply fall. This is illustrated in figure 4.2b.

Activity

In the following activity you are asked to consider the market for imported jeans. Using the demand and supply schedules below, sketch a graph of the curves and answer the following questions:

Price (£)	10	15	20	25	30	35	40
Quantity supplied (thousands)	20	40	75	90	120	150	180
Quantity demanded (thousands)	200	180	160	140	120	100	80

(i) What is the equilibrium price and level of output?

(ii) Assume supply increases by 55 units at every price due to a new production method. What would be the new equilibrium price and output?

(iii) What would happen to the jean supply curve if there was a cotton harvest failure?

(iv) In an attempt to encourage domestic jean manufacturers to produce more, the government fixes a jean import quota of 75 thousand pairs. What might be the implications of this action?

(v) A new fashion craze means that jeans are no longer in demand. Use demand and supply curves to show how both producers and consumers might respond to this situation.

(a) The equilibrium price is £30 and 120 thousand pairs are bought. (b) If supply increases by 50 units the new equilibrium price and output will be £25 and 140 thousand pairs. (c) The curve would shift left as the costs of production rise. (d) The implications of setting an import quota will be that the price of imported jeans will rise as they become short in supply. Domestically manufactured jeans now become more popular. (e) In figure 4.3 below note that demand initially shifts from D1 to D2 as jeans become less fashionable. As price falls suppliers look to shift their stocks fearing that prices may yet fall further. The supply curve shifts from S1 to S2 and prices fall further as a consequence.

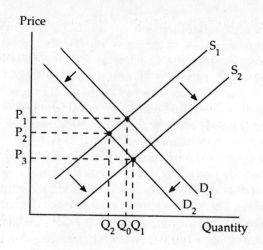

Figure 4.3 Shifts in demand and supply

4.4 The production decision: elasticity

Not only does a business want to know whether a price rise or fall will lead to a change in demand, but crucially they are concerned with how much. Will a price rise lead to a significant or minimal fall in the demand for their product or service? The term **elasticity** is used to describe the responsiveness of a change; in this case, of demand to a change in price. The more responsive demand is to a change in price the more price **elastic** is the good. A product or service that is unresponsive to a change in price is called **inelastic**. Whether the good or service is elastic or inelastic may depend upon a number of factors:

❑ the availability or closeness of substitutes – the more substitutes the more elastic;

❑ the proportion of income spent on the good – the larger the proportion the more elastic;

❑ the period of time over which consumer decisions are allowed to change -the longer the time the more elastic.

One of the most important applications of elasticity concerns the relationship between a change in price and its effect on the organisations sales revenue.

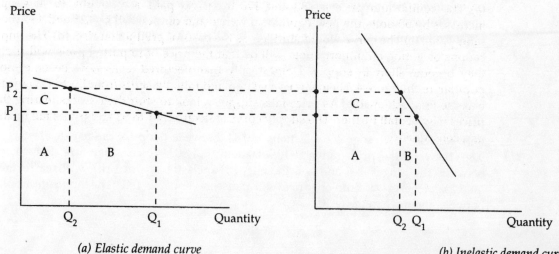

(a) Elastic demand curve

(b) Inelastic demand curve
Figure 4.4 Elasticity and total revenue

In Figure 4.4 we have two demand curves. In (a) the curve represents a good that is price elastic in demand, in (b) the curve represents a good that is price inelastic. In (a) prior to a price increase the firms total revenue (TR) is equal to areas A and B. Following a rise in price the new TR area is equal to A and C. Area B is greater than area C thus showing that the price rise has led to a fall in revenue. With an elastic demand curve, price and total revenue will move in opposite directions. Alternatively with an inelastic demand curve, as price rises then total revenue rises. In this case price and total revenue move in the same direction.

Even if we could estimate the demand curve for a product, to simply look at the curve may not fully reveal the goods elasticity. This is particularly true when we are analysing a product whose elasticity varies along its length (most demand curves are not straight lines). Therefore a simple mathematical technique can be used to estimate an elasticity coefficient, the value of which tells us whether the product is elastic or inelastic and the strength of this condition.

$$\text{The price elasticity of demand} = \frac{\text{proportionate or percentage change in Q}}{\text{proportionate or percentage change in P}}$$

A proportionate change in Q is measured by dividing the change in Q by Q, i.e. $\Delta Q/Q$.

A proportionate change in P is measured by dividing the change in P by P, i.e. $\Delta P/P$.

where Δ means 'change in'

Thus price elasticity of demand can be calculated using the following formula:

$$\frac{\Delta Q}{Q} \div \frac{\Delta P}{P}$$

Using this formula, a value greater than 1 illustrates an elastic demand curve, whereas a value less than 1 shows an inelastic demand curve.

Activity

Using the table of values below, calculate the elasticity of demand for each of the price ranges. From your results indicate whether the curve is elastic or inelastic, and assess the impact such a price change would have on the organisation's total revenue. Double check your expectations by calculating total revenue in each case.

P(£)	4	6	8	10
Q	45	35	25	15

Between the price range 4–6, elasticity = 0.44. Between the price range 6–8, elasticity = 0.88. Between the price range 8–10, elasticity = 1.60. We can therefore deduce that between the ranges 4–6 and 6–8 the curve is inelastic. A price rise will see revenue increase, whereas a drop in price will cause revenue to fall. The opposite applies between the price range 8–10.

4.5   More on elasticity

As well as price elasticity of demand, the concept of elasticity can be used to assess the responsiveness of demand to factors other than price.

Cross price elasticity of demand measures the responsiveness of demand for one good in respect to a change in the price of another good. Such a measure is useful when dealing with goods that have close complements or substitutes.

Income elasticity of demand measures the responsiveness of demand to a change in income. The most important determinant of income elasticity is the degree to which the good is a necessity. The more a necessity, the lower the income elasticity. If the income elasticity becomes negative then the good is identified as being **inferior**. That is as incomes rise people buy less of it, shifting consumption to what may be perceived as superior products.

Activity

The data below shows estimated values of income elasticities for various foods. Are you surprised at the findings?

Milk	−0.40
Margarine	−0.44
Potatoes	−0.48
Sugar	−0.54
Bread	−0.25
Cakes and biscuits	0.02
Tea	−0.56
Coffee	0.23
Cheese	0.19
Fruit juice	0.94
Fresh vegetables	0.35

You should not be surprised at what the figures suggest. As income rises, demand for those foods with a negative income elasticity will fall. These goods are considered inferior. Slightly more luxury goods such as cake and coffee will rise when income increases.

Summary

We have identified in this chapter three principal factors a business might consider prior to producing its good or service; namely demand, supply and the concept of elasticity. In order to enhance a businesses chances of economic success, as well as these factors, careful consideration will need to be given to business costs which are considered in the next chapter.

Further reading

Sloman J, *Economics*, Harvester Wheatsheaf, 1994, Chapter 3 Sections 3.1 to 3.5.

Sloman J and Sutcliffe M, *Economics Workbook*, Harvester Wheatsheaf, 1994, Chapter 3 selectively

Dunnet A, *Understanding the Market* Longman, 1992, Chapters 2 and 4

Progress questions

1. The demand curve of a business is represented by a simple **inverse/direct** relationship between price and quantity.

2. The supply curve of a business is represented by a simple **inverse/direct** relationship between price and quantity.

3. List six factors that will cause the **demand** curve to shift: ....
   ....

4. List four factors that will cause the supply curve to shift: ....
   ....

5. A market equilibrium is when: ....

6. An elastic good is one that is: ....

7. An inelastic good is one that is: ....

8. A value of 0.3 signifies an elastic demand. True ☐ False ☐

9. Cross price elasticity of demand measures: ....
   ....

10. A negative income elasticity of demand shows that the good is normal.
    True ☐ False ☐

Review questions

11. Outline the main differences between traditional consumer theory and modern consumer theory. (Section 4.2)

12. Explain, using relevant diagrams, why certain factors cause the demand and supply curves to shift. (Section 4.2 and 4.3)

13. Why is an understanding of elasticity important to the business manager? (Section 4.4)

14. Explain how we can calculate the elasticity of demand for a particular good. (Section 4.4)

15. How might cross price and income elasticity of demand be of value to the business organization? (Section 4.5)

Multiple choice questions

16. Which of the following will cause the demand curve for cars to shift right:
    (a) consumer income falls.
    (b) the price of petrol rises.
    (c) the cost of public transport rises.
    (d) public awareness of pollution damage from cars grows.

17. If it is expected that the price charged of future output will rise, then;
    (a) the supply curve will shift left.
    (b) the supply curve will shift right.
    (c) more information is need to decide what will happen to the supply curve.
    (d) there will be a movement down the supply curve.

18. An inferior good is one that:
    (a) has a positive income elasticity value.
    (b) is not a necessity.
    (c) has a negative income elasticity value.
    (d) has few substitutes.

Practice questions

19. Explain why, through the free play of demand and supply, the market will always tend towards equilibrium.

20. Explain the relationship between price elasticity of demand and profit.

21. Why are businesses unlikely to know the price elasticity of demand for their product? How might they discover such information?

Assignment

The aim of this assignment is to investigate consumer demand and how it might change. Conduct an interview with a family you know. Ask them to list what they might normally purchase in a week and how much each item roughly costs. Then ask your respondents how their purchases might change if the income they allocated to shopping increased by 50%. From this information calculate the income elasticity of demand for certain products and identify any products that we can classify as inferior goods.

5   Business costs and market prices

5.1   Introduction

As we have mentioned in Chapter 3 the traditional view of the firm assumes that it will attempt to maximise profits. In order to achieve this goal the business will require information concerning its cost and revenue structure. On completing this chapter you should be able to:

❏ distinguish between fixed, variable, average and marginal costs;

❏ explain the implications of the long run on a businesses cost structure;

❏ distinguish between average and marginal revenue;

❏ locate the point of profit maximisation;

❏ identify the profit made at the profit maximising point;

❏ describe how prices are set in the real world.

5.2.   The short run and the long run

A business organisations costs are directly related to the factors of production it uses to produce a given level of output. We can distinguish between;

❏ **fixed factors**, which cannot be increased in supply over a given period of time, such as building a factory, and;

❏ **variable factors**, which can be increased in supply over a given time period, such as the employment of additional workers.

This distinction enables us to identify between the firms **short run** and **long run** position.

❏ The short run is a period of time in which at least one factor of production is fixed in supply and as such output can only be increased by adding more variable factors of production.

❏ The long run is a period of time in which all the factors of production are variable.

Activity

What would be the effect, over a period time, of progressively adding more of a variable factor of production, such as labour, to a fixed factor such as land?

The consequence of adding more of a variable factor such as labour to a fixed factor such as land, is that the additional output per worker, while initially rising, will over time fall as the land becomes more crowded and the possibility of achieving greater output from the land declines. This is known as the **law of diminishing returns**. Stated simply, it means that the output achieved from adding an additional unit of the variable factor will be less than that achieved from the previous unit. Hence only in the long run, when all factors are variable, can the business avoid diminishing returns.

5.3 Total, average and marginal costs

As mentioned previously a firm's costs will be determined by the factors of production it uses. Fixed factors of production such as land will constitute a **fixed cost** in so far as the rent paid on the land will not vary with the level of output. Alternatively variable factors of production such as labour will constitute a **variable cost,** as the more produced will lead to more workers being employed, and hence the higher the cost.
Given such costs we can identify:

❑ **total costs (TC),** which are the sum of the business's total fixed costs (FC) and variable costs (VC).

$$TC = FC + VC$$

❑ **average cost (AC),** which represent the cost per unit of production and can be found by dividing the total costs of production by the quantity produced (Q).

$$AC = \frac{TC}{Q}$$

❑ **marginal cost (MC),** which are the costs incurred from producing one additional unit of production, can be found by dividing the change in total costs by the change in quantity.

$$MC = \frac{\Delta TC}{\Delta Q}$$

Using a numerical example a business's cost might look like the following:

Q	FC	VC	TC	AC	MC
0	10	0	10	0	
1	10	5	15	15	5
2	10	8	18	9	3
3	10	11	21	7	3
4	10	18	28	7	7
5	10	30	40	8	12
6	10	50	60	10	15

We can see from the figures that total costs rise the more units that are produced. We can also see that average costs and marginal costs change with the level of output. Both fall then rise as the level of production increases. If we plot average and marginal costs as shown in figure 5.1 we can observe that the marginal cost curve cuts the average cost curve at its lowest point. This identifies the most efficient point of production. Any point to the left of point x will mean that additional output costs less than the average and hence the average must be falling. Whereas any point to the right indicates that the additional units of production cost more than the average and hence the average must be rising.

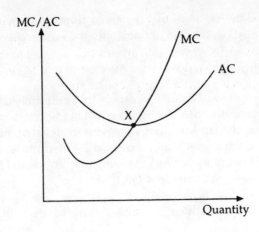

Figure 5.1 Marginal and average costs

Businesses will observe that the more they produce the lower their average costs per unit become. This means that the firm is experiencing growing economies of scale. Beyond the point where the average cost curve is cut by the marginal cost curve, the average costs per unit will begin to rise, hence the business is experiencing diseconomies of scale.

5.4   Total, average and marginal revenue

In order to locate the profit maximising level of output, in addition to the cost curves we need to analyse the businesses revenue curves. When looking at revenue we need to distinguish between:

❑ **Total revenue (TR)**, which is the total earnings from a particular level of output. This is found by multiplying price (P) by quantity (Q).

$$TR = P \times Q$$

❑ **Average revenue (AR)** which is the amount the business earns from each unit of output. This is simply the goods price.

$$AR = \frac{TR}{Q} \text{ or } AR = P$$

❑ **Marginal revenue (MR)** which is the additional revenue from producing one more unit of the product, and can be found by dividing the change in the business's total revenue by the change in quantity.

$$MR = \frac{\Delta TR}{\Delta Q}$$

Before we can offer a numerical example to illustrate the business's revenue curves, it should be noted that if the business's price does not vary with output (the smaller the firm the more likely this is) then the average revenue curve will be a straight line. The average revenue curve in this case will also represent the marginal revenue curve, since one more unit sold will simply add that amount to total revenue.

Alternatively if price does vary with output (the larger the firm the more likely this is) then the following example might be offered.

Q	P = AR	TR	MR
1	10	10	
2	9	18	8
3	8	24	6
4	7	28	4
5	6	30	2
6	5	30	0

We can see from the above illustration that as the price per unit is lowered to sell more output, then average revenue will fall. We can also note that marginal revenue will be less than average revenue due to the fact that the price, when reduced, must be reduced on all the units sold, not just the extra unit. In figure 5.2a we can see the average and marginal revenue curves of a business where price varies with output. In contrast figure 5.2b illustrates a situation where the firm is a price taker and the price is determined by the market.

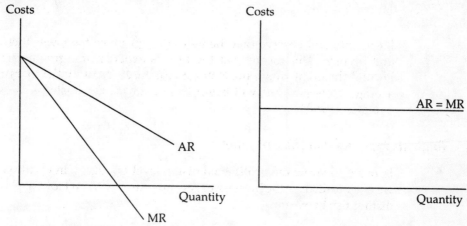

Figure 5.2a Average and marginal
revenue where price varies with output

Figure 5.2b Average and marginal
revenue where the firm is a price taker

Figure 5.2 Average and marginal revenue

Activity

In sections 5.3 and 5.4 we have identified the businesses costs and revenue structure. Before we reveal how we might show the maximisation of profits given such information, consider this problem for yourself. Before considering your answer note that there are two possible alternatives, one involves the use of the total curves, the other the average and marginal curves. Once you have attempted this problem read section 5.5 to reveal the answers.

5.5   Profit maximisation

Once the business has collected data on its cost and revenue structure it can then set about maximising its profits. Profit maximisation can be identified in two ways:

❑ using total cost and total revenue;

❑ using average and marginal cost and average and marginal revenue.

Taking the total cost and total revenue data from sections 5.3 and 5.4 above we have the following:

Q	TC	TR	Total Profit
0	10	0	−10
1	15	10	−5
2	18	18	0
3	21	24	3
4	28	28	0
5	40	30	−10
6	60	30	−30

Where profits are negative the firm is clearly making a loss. The greatest gap between total revenue and total cost is at a level of 3 units of output. This is shown graphically in figure 5.3 below.

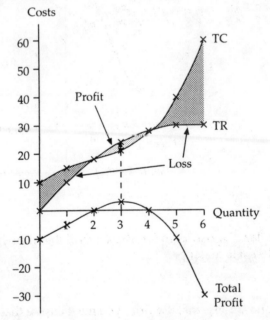

Figure 5.3 Profit maximisation using total costs and total revenue curves

In using the average and marginal cost and revenue curves to illustrate profit maximisation, we must first locate the profit maximisation level of output, and then identify how much profit is made at this point. In order to locate the profit maximisation level of output we look for the point where marginal costs equal marginal revenue. Here the additional cost of one more unit is equal to the revenue gained. If one more unit is produced then the additional cost of this one unit will exceed revenue from its sale. Using the data from sections 5.3 and 5.4 we can show the profit maximising level of output.

Q	AC	MC	AR	MR
0	0		0	
1	15	5	10	0
2	9	3	9	8
3	7	3	8	6
4	7	7	7	4
5	8	12	6	2
6	10	15	5	0

Once we have located the profit maximising level of output we must then measure the amount of profit made at this point. To do this we need to add the average cost and average revenue curves. This will tell us how much profit is made on the sale of the maximising unit of production. To find total profit we simply multiply this amount by the number of units sold. This is represented by the shaded area in figure 5.4 below.

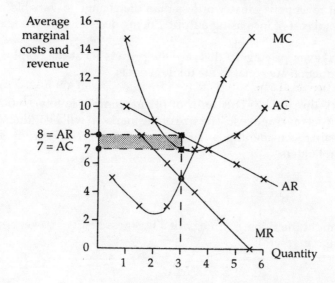

Figure 5.4 Profit maximisation using average and marginal curves

Activity

Using a similar diagram as in 5.4, show a firm that is making a loss and highlight the size of loss it is making.

In order to show a loss making firm, you must ensure that the average cost curve is at all points above the average revenue curve. The loss rather than profit at this point can be highlighted in a similar manner to that shown in figure 5.4.

5.6 Pricing in the real world

It is often argued that the theoretical model detailed above, known as marginal cost pricing, in which the firm attempts to maximise profits through a consideration of its marginal costs and marginal revenue, lacks realism. Three major problems of realism are that:

❏ not all firms might attempt to maximise profits, as detailed in chapter 3 section 3.4. Alternative business goals might be sought such as high investment or growth;

❏ businesses may not have sufficient **information** to calculate their marginal costs and revenue;

❏ markets are constantly changing in response to many factors, prices must be adjusted as a response to such fluctuations. In certain instances prices may be set on anticipated future demand.

Three alternative, and possibly more realistic pricing strategies that we might consider are:

❏ **incremental pricing**. Prices are set in this case by considering whether the change in total revenue is greater or less than the change in variable costs, that is the incremental cost of increasing output. Pricing decisions are not taken at the margin;

❏ **breakeven pricing**. In this case the price is set at the point where the total costs of production are equal to the total revenue;

❏ **mark-up pricing**. This form of pricing simply involves adding a mark-up to the products average cost. The size of the mark-up will be influenced by a wide range of possible considerations such as what level of profit is needed to satisfy shareholders.

Activity

How might the pricing strategy of a business be used to keep new firms out of a particular market?

Firms can use price setting as a **barrier to entry**. By reducing their price, an established firm can drive potential new entrants out of the market. The length of time that such a strategy could be maintained will depend upon the business's financial position and whether or not it is making a loss as a consequence of its low price policy. Such a business strategy is known as **predatory pricing**.

5.7   Pricing and the product life cycle

All products have a life cycle. The phases of a typical life cycle are shown in figure 5.5.

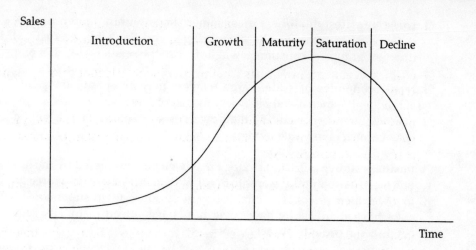

Figure 5.5 The product life cycle

Over the various phases of the cycle businesses may adopt distinct pricing strategies. When the product first enters the market two alternative strategies will present themselves;

❐ **penetration pricing**. Here the business could set a very low price, possibly no more than breaking-even, this will enable the firm to rapidly create a market for its new product. Such a pricing strategy will usually be adopted where significant cost reductions might be gained from higher levels of production in the long run;

❐ **market skimming pricing**. Here the business will set a very high initial price to maximise returns. As competitors enter the market the price will be reduced. The more the producer has a monopoly position in the market, the more likely this form of pricing will occur.

Activity

What pricing strategy might a business adopt at the growth, maturity and saturation stages of the product life cycle?

During the growth and maturity stages of the cycle the business will be looking to maximise profits and have a high price mark-up. As the market nears saturation and eventually decline, the pricing strategy of the business will aim to maintain demand and retain profits through the volume of sales it makes rather than by operating a high profit margin. As such the business may look to reduce its price.

5.8 The consumer and prices

By the time that most products get to the consumer, usually via a retailer, the product has not only received the manufacturers mark-up but the distributor's mark-up as well. The price charged may far exceed the initial costs of production. The final price that the consumer pays ultimately rests with the retailer, who may or may not sell the product at the manufacturers recommended price. Three factors that might influence the retailers decision are:

41

❑ **consumer lifestyle**. Where a consumer shops within a town or city; whether the consumer has access to alternative shops; and the price elasticity of demand for different groups of consumers will influence the retailers decision on price.

❑ **retail economies of scale**. Large retailers may be able to lower their prices and subsequently increase their sales, by negotiating advantageous prices from the manufacturer, hence cutting their own costs. Smaller retailers will be less likely to achieve such favourable terms.

❑ **business strategy**. Pricing strategy may well be determined by the level of competition faced. Attempts by stores to boost their market share may force rival businesses to lower their prices. The establishment of out-of-town superstores; who in many cases have significantly lower over-heads, has forced many city centre retailers to cut prices in order to attract custom.

Activity

How might a small corner shop that sells groceries stay in business when faced with the significantly lower prices that a large supermarket might charge?

The answer to this problem does not lie in the smaller grocer attempting to cut cost. On cost criteria the supermarket will be more successful. The grocer, in order to remain in business will need to provide a quality service, not only in respect of product quality but, for example, free home delivery. Other aspects of service such as opening hours and the diversification of product ranges might be necessary.

Summary

In this chapter we have considered how a firm might set about maximising its level of profits. We have also considered a range of alternative pricing methods that could be adopted, and how pricing strategy will be influenced not only by a products life cycle but also reflect the concerns of the retailer.

Further reading

Sloman J, *Economics*, Harvester Wheatsheaf, 1994, Chapter 5 (for advanced students only).

Dunnet A, *Understanding the Market* Longman, 1992, Chapter 5 and 6.

Progress questions

1. Distinguish between the short run and long run: ....

   ....

2. Average costs will always cut marginal costs at their lowest point.

   True ☐ False ☐

3. Total costs = ...

4. The average revenue curve is equal to price because: ....
....

5. When total revenue is equal to total costs, profits are maximised.

    True ☐ False ☐

6. At the point where MC = MR the business will know: ....
....

7. Give three reasons why marginal cost pricing lacks realism: ....
....

8. Give three alternative pricing strategies the business might adopt: ....
....

9. A market skimming strategy means starting with a low price for a new product.

    True ☐ False ☐

10. Give three factors that might influence the price charged to the consumer by the
retailer: ....
....

Review questions

11. Given only fixed and variable costs, show how it is possible to calculate the business's total, average and marginal costs. (Section 5.2 and 5.3)

12. Illustrate how a business might maximise its profits using total revenue and total cost curves.(Section 5.2 and 5.5)

13. Illustrate how a business might maximise its profits using average and marginal curves.(Section 5.2 and 5.5)

14. What will influence the price charged by a business when deciding to launch a new product?(Section 5.7)

15. How will the level of competition faced by both the business and the retailer influence its pricing strategy?(Section 5.8)

Multiple choice questions

16. The long run can be distinguished from the short run by;
    (a) all factors of production being variable.
    (b) a rise in business output.
    (c) the law of diminishing returns.
    (d) the rising opportunity cost of labour.

17. Profit maximisation can be identified where:

    (a) Marginal cost cuts average cost at its lowest point.

    (b) Total revenue is at its highest point.

    (c) Marginal revenue is equal to marginal cost.

    (d) Total cost is at its lowest.

18. Marginal cost pricing is unrealistic because:

    (a) Businesses do not have adequate information.

    (b) Profit maximisation might not be a business goal.

    (c) Prices are set largely in response to changing market conditions.

    (d) All of the above.

Practice questions

19. Explain and illustrate how a business might maximise its profits.

20. What factors will influence the setting of prices in the real world other than production costs?

21. How might government policy influence both business costs and the price that businesses might set?

Assignment

The deregulation of bus transport has had a significant effect upon the level of competition within the market and the fare prices charged. Conduct an investigation into your local bus service. See whether competition has increased and assess the impact this competition has had upon fare prices. Also consider the routes that bus operators run, and assess whether the price differences reflect distinct aspects of each market segment.

6 Market structure and the conduct of business

6.1 Introduction

The level of competition a business faces has an important influence over its decision-making considerations. For example, what price to set, what level of output to produce, whether to innovate with new products or to embark upon an aggressive advertising campaign. In this chapter we will look at how market structure influences the conduct of business and subsequently shapes its performance.

On completing this chapter you should be able to:

❒ distinguish between alternative market structures;

❒ outline the key features of perfect competition, monopoly, monopolistic competition and oligopoly;

❒ appreciate the relevance that market structure has in influencing business decisions.

6.2 Identifying market structures

Four distinct market structures can be determined on the basis of the level of competition. The level of competition that a business faces will be highly significant in shaping the actions and strategy it pursues. These four market structures are:

❒ **perfect competition**;

❒ **monopolistic competition**;

❒ **oligopoly**;

❒ **monopoly**.

It is common to further distinguish between such market structures by considering three additional criteria:

❒ whether there are **barriers to entry** preventing new firms entering the market;

❒ whether the product produced differs between firms or whether it is largely identical;

❒ whether the business can exert control over the products price, that is, is it a price taker or a price setter.

In Figure 6.1 we can see how the four market structures differ from one another in respect to the above criteria.

Type of market	Number of firms	Freedom of entry	Nature of product	Examples	Implication for demand curve of firm
Perfect competition	Very many	Unrestricted	Homogeneous (undifferentiated)	Cabbages, carrots (these approximate to perfect competition)	Horizontal. The firm is a price taker
Monopolistic competition	Many/ several	Unrestricted	Differentiated	Plumbers, restaurants	Downward sloping, but relatively elastic. The firm has some control over price
Oligopoly	Few	Restricted	1. Undifferentiated or 2. Differentiated	1. Cement 2. Cars, electrical appliances	Downward sloping, relatively inelastic but depends on reactions of rivals to a price change
Monopoly	One	Restricted or completely blocked	Unique	British Gas, local bus service (in many towns)	Downward sloping, more inelastic than oligopoly. Firm has considerable control over price

Figure 6.1 Distinguishing between alternative market structures

Activity

The market structures identified above represent theoretical models which are general approximations to reality. Given that all markets in many respects may be unique, what value are such models to the business economist?

Such models are based upon a series of narrow assumptions concerning how the real world operates, they do not represent the world as it is. The purpose of such models is to help us predict how businesses might behave when placed within distinct market environments. They offer us no more than a general guide to business behaviour.

6.3   Perfect competition

A perfectly competitive market has the following characteristics:

☐ a large number of business organisations;

☐ each business only produces a small fraction of the industry's total output;

☐ businesses are price takers;

☐ there are no barriers to entry preventing new businesses coming into the market;

☐ all firms in the industry produce an identical product, there is no branding or advertising;

☐ producers and consumers are assumed to have perfect knowledge.

Very few markets achieve this ideal, although certain agricultural markets come close to it. The use of the perfectly competitive model is as an **ideal type**, and hence a basis to assess how real world markets deviate from such an ideal.

When considering this market structure we need to distinguish between the businesses short run and long run position. In the short run, as shown in figure 6.2, we assume that the firm will attempt to maximise profits by equating marginal revenue (MR) equal to marginal costs (MC), this will lead to the production of a level of output Q_e. Given that the firm has no control over the market price, the businesses demand or average revenue curve (AR) is horizontal at this price. This price will also reflect the businesses MR curve, given that the price received by the business is not affected by how much it produces.

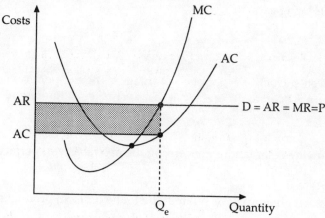

Figure 6.2 Short run profit maximisation in a perfectly competitive market

As figure 6.2 shows, the average cost curve (AC) dips below the AR curve. The firm is now earning **supernormal profits**. Supernormal profits differ from **normal profits** in so far as the cost curves are assumed to include a given return on capital investment sufficient to keep the business in the market. New firms will now, in response to the supernormal profits, be attracted to this industry. Given that there are no barriers to entry, new firms will set up in business and cause the total level of supply within the market to rise. Hence in the long run the market price will fall to the point where firms are making only normal profits (figure 6.3). If supply increased such that prices fell even further, such that business made a loss, then as businesses left the market prices would once again start to rise.

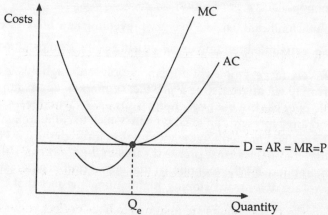

Figure 6.3 Long run equilibrium in a perfectly competitive market

What is so perfect about perfect competition? The following advantages might be identified:

- competition will force firms to be efficient or go out of business;

- in the long run the business will operate at the lowest point on its average costs curve;

- the consumer gains from low prices in the long run as there are no supernormal profits being earned.

Activity

Even given such clear economic advantages whether perfect competition is desirable or not is open to debate. What disadvantages or limitations might it create?

The following reservations concerning the desirability of perfect competition might be raised:

- consumer choice will be limited due to the uniform product produced;

- economies of scale will be difficult to achieve;

- without supernormal profits businesses may find it difficult to invest in new technology or research new products.

6.4 Monopoly

When we describe a market structure as a monopoly it will have the following characteristics:

- there is only one business organisation;
- its demand curve is the industry's demand curve;
- the monopolist is a price setter;
- there are significant barriers to entry preventing new businesses entering the market;
- there is very little branding or advertising as the firm produces a single product.

There are very few examples of pure monopoly, although this is largely determined by how narrowly we might define a product or market. For example, British Gas have a monopoly over gas but not over energy sources. As with the model of perfect competition monopoly represents an ideal type by which to compare reality.

Unlike perfect competition the monopolist, through the use of barriers to entry, will ensure that the supernormal profits it earns in the short run will be maintained in the long run. In figure 6.4 the monopolist maximises profits where MR = MC. The AR and MR curves are downward sloping highlighting the fact that changes in output will influence the price charged.

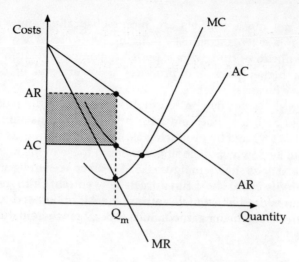

Figure 6.4 Profit maximising under monopoly

It may be argued that monopolistic market structures have the following advantages:

❒ the monopolist may gain significant economies of scale;

❒ a monopolist may have lower costs due to enhanced efficiency from investment;

❒ monopolists may be able to diversify their product ranges and introduce new products due to the supernormal profits they might earn.

Activity

Despite the above, monopolies are frequently seen as a bad thing. Why might this be the case?

The following might be seen as problems stemming from monopoly market structures:

❒ monopolies may suffer from inefficiency due to a lack of competition;

❒ monopolies will charge a higher price and produce less output than markets which are more competitive;

❒ monopolies exert market power and may operate in the interest of one group in society at the expense of others.

6.5 Monopolistic competition

A monopolistically competitive industry has the following characteristics:

❒ there are a large number of business organisations;

❒ each business has only a small share of the market;

❒ there is freedom of entry into the industry;

❒ businesses produce distinct products from their rivals;

❒ monopolistically competitive businesses have a downward sloping demand curve (elastic) which gives them some control over the price of the product they sell.

Many, if not most, markets are monopolistically competitive, especially those in retailing; newsagents, chemists, building firms etc. When we compare a monopolistically competitive firm with a perfectly competitive firm we find that the former charges a higher price and produces a lower level of output than the perfectly competitive business.

We can show this by considering the position of the monopolistically competitive business in both the short and long run. The firm maximises its profits at the point where MR = MC, and by producing a differentiated product the business's AR and MR curves will be downward sloping, similar to those of the monopolist, only they will be far more elastic as shown in figure 6.5. As can be seen in figure 6.6 the earning of super-normal profits in the short run attracts new entrants into the market. Demand for the existing firms product will fall, causing the AR or demand curve to shift left until only normal profits are being earned. Such a point is where the AR curve is tangent to the AC curve.

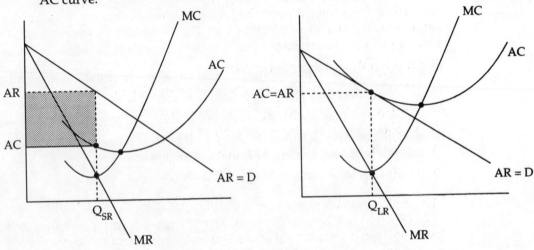

Figure 6.5 Short run profit maximisation under monopolistic competition

Figure 6.6 Long run profit maximisation under monopolistic competition

If you compare this to figure 6.2 in the long run, you will observe that the perfectly competitive firm will produce more output and charge a lower price, as well as operate at a lower more efficient point on the AC curve.

Activity

What advantages are to be gained by the consumer from the monopolistically competitive market structure?

The principal benefit can be found in wider consumer choice. The fact that products are differentiated and subsequently vary in design, quality and other non-price factors may off-set the lower price perfectly competitive markets might offer.

6.6 Oligopoly

Oligopolistic industries have the following characteristics:

❏ there are few business organisations in the industry;

❏ each business has a significant market share, although such shares need not be equal;

❏ there are barriers to entry preventing new businesses entering the market;

❏ businesses can produce distinct products from their rivals and spend large amounts on advertising and branding;

❏ oligopolistic businesses are **interdependent** and must take account of their rival's actions when making decisions;

❏ oligopolistic businesses face an inelastic demand curve and have a high degree of control over the price of their product.

The behaviour of oligopolistic industries is the most difficult to predict. This is due to the variety of ways that businesses might respond to changes in the economic environment that they face. The uncertainty that oligopolistic businesses might face can be reduced by collusion, either in the form of a cartel or through more tacit or informal agreements if cartels are against the law. The possibility of successful collusion within a market will be influenced by:

❏ the fewer the number of businesses;

❏ the lack of secrecy concerning costs and production methods;

❏ whether the oligopolists have similar cost and revenue structures;

❏ the potential threat of new entrants into the market;

❏ the stability of the market, such that it does not fluctuate greatly with demand;

❏ the attitude of government to the affairs of business.

The pricing and output decision of the oligopolist will be determined by whether it is in a collusive or competitive market. Therefore unlike the other market structures we have considered there are in fact many models of oligopolistic business behaviour, the predictions of such models are determined by the assumptions we might make concerning the businesses relations with its rivals.

A formal collusive agreement between oligopolistic businesses is known as a **cartel**. The cartel will act as though it were a single firm or a monopoly. If such formal agreements are against the law, as they are in the UK and EU, then collusion may be **tacit** or informal. One such model of tacit collusion is known as **price leadership**. Price leadership might be of two types:

❏ from a **dominant business**. Here the dominant business, usually determined by its market share, sets its price during the normal process of maximising profits. The price it sets is then followed by its smaller rivals.

❏ from a **barometric business**, that is a business that responds best to changes in the business environment. It is assumed that the actions of this business will be in the interests of all its rivals, so they all set prices at similar levels.

If collusion breaks down the behaviour of oligopolistic businesses becomes very difficult to predict. Their actions are now largely determined by what they think their rivals may do if faced, with for example, a cut in price. Will they respond with a cut in price themselves? Will they launch an adverting campaign to win back business? Businesses are now forced to consider their **business strategy**, that is the means by which they intend to remain competitive. They need to consider how they in turn will react once their rivals have acted. The possibilities may be endless, particularly so if the oligopolistic industry contains a large number of firms each with a significant market share.

Given such uncertainty it is hardly surprising that oligopolistic markets appear overtime to be very stable, even when little or no collusion exists. **The kinked demand curve theory** of oligopoly assumes that;

❏ if an oligopolist cuts its price, then its rivals will be forced to follow suit. Hence a fall in price will lead to the business attracting very few new customers. Demand will be inelastic.

❏ if an oligopolist raises its price, then its rival will not follow suit. Hence a price rise will lead to a large fall in customers as they shift their consumption to a cheaper alternative. Demand will in this case be elastic.

The implications of this can be seen in figure 6.7. Price stability will be maintained at the point where the demand curve is kinked.

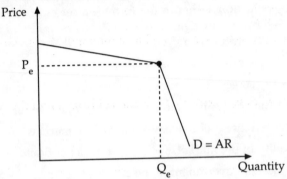

Figure 6.7 The kinked demand curve

Activity

Even though businesses may collude over certain aspects of business policy, such as what price to charge, they may still compete on non-price terms. What forms might such non-price competition take?

The two major areas of non-price competition you might identify are **product development** and **advertising**.

Product development is an attempt to produce a product clearly distinct from the business's main rivals. Advertising aims to increase sales of a brand and also increase brand loyalty.

Summary

The four market structures that we have outlined above enable us to assess and predict how a business might behave when faced with alternative competitive environments. Oligopolistic markets in particular are very difficult to predict, and this is reflected in the variety of alternative models we might consider.

Further reading

Sloman J, *Economics*, Harvester Wheatsheaf, 1994, Chapter 6 Sections 6.1 – 6.3, Chapter 7 Sections 7.1 and 7.2.

Progress questions

1. The four main market structures identified in economics are: ....

    ....

2. In perfect competition businesses are price setters.   True ☐ False ☐

3. In order for perfect competition to operate consumers must have perfect knowledge.

    True ☐ False ☐

4. Distinguish between normal and supernormal profits: ....

    ....

5. Whether a business is defined as a monopolist depends upon how we define the market.

    True ☐ False ☐

6. Three advantages that might be gained from a monopoly market structure are:

    ....

    ....

7. A monopolistically competitive market structure will not have barriers to entry.

    True ☐ False ☐

8. Non-price competition is an important part of oligopolistic business.

    True ☐ False ☐

9. Six factors that favour collusion between oligopolistic businesses are:

    ....

    ....

10. A barometric price leader is a business: ....

    ....

Review questions

11. How does a perfectly competitive market differ from a monopolistically competitive market? (Section 6.2, 6.3 and 6.5)

12. Make a case both for and against a monopoly market structure. (Section 6.4)

13. Why is the interdependence of oligopolistic businesses so important in shaping their business strategy? (Section 6.6)

14. What are the advantages of advertising both for the business and the consumer? (Section 6.6)

15. What is the kinked demand curve and what does it tell us about oligopolistic market structures? (Section 6.6)

Multiple choice questions

16. Which of the following is **not** a characteristic of a perfectly competitive market;
    (a) businesses are price takers.
    (b) economic decision makers have perfect knowledge.
    (c) there are barriers to entry.
    (d) there is no advertising.

17. Which of the following is **not** seen as an advantage of a monopoly market structure?
    (a) producers can make supernormal profits.
    (b) lower costs.
    (c) economies of scale.
    (d) R&D and product development.

18. The kinked demand curve theory of oligopoly assumes that;
    (a) all oligopolist in a particular market will copy their rivals price changes.
    (b) a rise in price will be copied but a price cut will not.
    (c) a rise in price will not be copied but a price cut will.
    (d) all oligopolist are independent of their rivals and will not respond to changes in price.

Practice questions

19. Why do economists distinguish between alternative market structures? Give examples of how alternative markets might be identified.

20. What value is there in studying perfect competition and monopoly when as market structures they do not exist?

21. "The behaviour of oligopolistic business is impossible to predict." Discuss.

Assignment

Conduct an investigation into a well known industry and determine from the information you collect what type of market structure it appears to have. Identify its key defining characteristics and assess how such characteristics might influence its business strategy. You are advised to select an industry where information is not likely to be to difficult to find.

7   *Small firms and multinationals*

7.1   Introduction

In the previous chapter we considered models of alternative market structures. In this chapter we will look at the economic role played by both small firms and multinational companies in the UK economy. Both types of business organization bring with them not only distinct economic advantages but also distinct economic limitations.

On completing this chapter you should be able to:

❐ outline the difficulties in defining and measuring the small firm sector;

❐ list the advantages and disadvantages of being a small firm;

❐ describe a range of government policies used to expand and improve the performance of the small firm sector;

❐ define and distinguish between different multinationals;

❐ list the main reasons why businesses go multinational;

❐ outline the costs and benefits of multinational investment on the economy.

7.2   Small firms and the UK economy

The Bolton Committee Report (1971) suggested that an economic definition of a small firm should have the following three criteria:

❐ it should have a small market share;

❐ it should be managed by its owner;

❐ it should not be part of a larger business organisation, such that it can make its own business decisions.

For statistical purposes however, such criteria would be very difficult to use. There is no agreed statistical definition as to exactly how small a small firm is. Most surveys tend to focus upon the number of employees within the firm. The size of a small firm, if we use the level of employment, is found to vary between industrial sectors. A small manufacturing firm may employ 200 people, whereas a small construction firm may employee no more than 25.

The problems we encounter in defining the small firm make it very difficult to calculate its importance as a form of business organization within the economy. This is made even more so due to the fact that government statistics may seriously underestimate the number of small firms. Two reasons for this are:

❐ firms smaller than 20 employees need not complete the **Census of Production** which government uses to monitor business structure and organization;

❐ firms who's turnover is small may be exempt from VAT registration. VAT registration is frequently used as an indicator of new business registration.

Even given the problems of definition and calculation the following table was compiled following a recent survey conducted on the structure of UK business by the size of employment.

Employment size band	Number of business (Thousands)	Share of total (per cent)		
		Business	Employment	Turnover
1–2	2,025	67.8	12.3	4.2
3–5	596	19.9	10.0	4.7
6–10	181	6.1	6.3	4.1
11–19	92	3.1	6.0	4.3
20–49	57	1.9	7.7	6.0
50–99	18	0.6	5.8	3.7
100–199	9	0.3	7.2	13.6
200–499	6	0.2	10.6	17.9
500–999	2	0.1	6.7	11.2
1,000+	1	0.0	27.5	30.4
Total	2,988	100.0	100.0	100.0

Source: Daly and McCann (1992)

Table 7.1 The size structure of UK business

Activity

How important is the small firm to the UK economy given the data in table 7.1? Assume that a typical small business is between 1-19 employees.

What we can deduce is that the small firm represents over 96.9% of all businesses, employing 34.6% of the labour force and contributing 17.3% of turnover. The small firm is without any doubt a very significant part of the business structure of the UK economy.

7.3 Small firms and competitiveness

The following have been found to be the key competitive advantages small firms might hold over their larger rivals:

❑ **flexibility**. Small firms are more able to respond to changes in the market and more effectively meet customer requirements by, for example, developing or adapting products. Small firms may also be seen as more flexible in respect to making decisions quickly, avoiding the bureaucratic and formal decision making process that might exist in larger companies.

❑ **quality of service**. Small firms are more able to deal with customers in a personal manner, providing a more effective aftersales service.

❑ **production efficiency** and **low overhead costs**. Small firms may reduce cost and improve efficiency in a variety of ways: management that avoids waste; good labour relations; the employment of a highly skilled and motivated workforce; low accommodation costs.

❐ **product development**. Many small businesses operate in niche markets and produce products with very specific applications. The distinctiveness of the product they produce and the firms expertise is a source of competitiveness for the small business.

Activity

What economic problems are small firms likely to encounter?

The following have been found to hinder the economic performance of small firms:

❐ **selling** and **marketing**. Small firms face many problems in selling and marketing their products, this is particularly so in overseas markets. They are frequently seen, unlike large firms, to suffer from low credibility, stability and reliability. This problem may diminish as the small firm becomes more established and builds up its reputation.

❐ **funding R&D**. Many small firms, especially those developing products, may find it very difficult to attract sufficient backing for its ideas. Small businesses will frequently have little or no collateral and may be considered a highly risky investment.

❐ **management skills**. A crucial element in ensuring that small businesses not only survive but grow, is the quality of management. A lack of key management skills such as the ability to market a product effectively will act as a significant restraint on the businesses development.

❐ **economies of scale**. Small firms will have less opportunity to gain economies of scale and hence their costs may remain somewhat higher than their larger rivals (for a discussion of economies of scale see section 3.6).

7.4 Small firms and government assistance

Government policy aimed at the small firm sector has had three principle objectives. These are:

❐ to encourage individuals to **start up** their own businesses;

❐ to encourage small firms to **grow**;

❐ to offer advice and improve the **performance** of the small business sector.

Policies to encourage individuals to start their own businesses have focused upon offering financial incentives in the form of favourable tax rates and grants. Small firms face reduced rates of corporation tax, 25% rather than the standard rate of 33%. The **Enterprise Allowance Scheme** offers finance in the form of individual grants to those who wish to start their own business. Additional money can be received if the business is set up in an area that receives regional assistance. This is known as the **Enterprise Initiative**.

Policies to encourage small businesses to grow have largely focused upon the problems that small businesses face in raising finance. The **Loan Guarantee Scheme** introduced in 1981 was a government initiative which guaranteed up to 70% of a loan made by a bank to a small business, that either did not have sufficient collateral or was considered a high risk. The **Unlisted Securities Market** set up in 1980 gave small and medium size businesses easier access to venture capital on the London Stock Exchange.

In an attempt to improve the performance of small businesses, government has not only reduced its interference in respect to legislative requirements, such as small businesses being exempt from certain unfair dismissal procedures, it has attempted to provide advice to small businesses by setting up the **Local Enterprise Agencies**. These are privately run organizations that offer free advice and counselling to small businesses. There have also been initiatives to provide training for small businesses. The **Business Growth Training Programme** was set up in 1989 and aims to improve general business skills.

Activity

Table 7.2 below shows the finding taken from a survey carried out by the Small Business Research Centre in 1992. Given such findings how best might we argue that the small business sector could be helped by government?

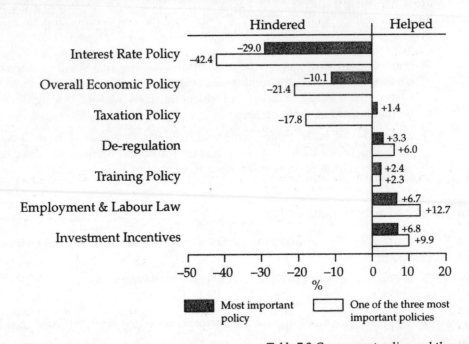

Table 7.2 Government policy and the small business

The findings suggest that most government initiatives aimed at the small business sector have tended on balance to have been beneficial. However, the two most significant factors affecting the performance of the small business are interest rate policy in particular, and economic policy in general, that is the governments handling of the economy. Such factors affect all business and not just small firms.

7.5 Multinationals and the UK economy

A multinational company (MNC) can be defined as one that owns or controls production or service facilities outside the country in which it is based. Such a definition is very general and mixes together MNC businesses that are very diverse. Multinationals differ in respect to:

❏ the number of overseas subsidiaries they might have;

❏ the size of an MNC's international operations relative to its overall operations;

❏ the number of countries in which subsidiaries are located;

❏ the type of business the MNC is involved in, whether extractive, industrial or based in the service sector;

❏ patterns of ownership and whether the MNC runs wholly owned subsidiaries or enters into joint ventures with foreign firms;

❏ business organization, whether all international operations are run from the home country or alternatively where overseas subsidiaries are run largely independently of the parent company.

Many of the larger multinationals have now grown to such a size that their earnings far exceed the GDP's of many countries. In 1989 General Motors had sales revenue that was three times as great as the GDP of New Zealand! In respect to the UK economy the tendency has been for investment by UK multinational to exceed the level of investment made by foreign multinationals in the UK. The largest single investor into the UK is the USA, accounting for 26.2% of total investment in 1990. Most investment into the UK has tended to focus upon manufacturing industry in high technology sectors of the economy, such as engineering and pharmaceuticals. Investment out of the UK has shifted in recent years from the USA to Europe and tends to focus on more lower tech areas of manufacture such as food production.

Activity

In table 7.3 we can see multinational investment both into and out of the UK since 1979. What does the data suggest?

	UK investment overseas	Overseas investment in the UK		UK investment overseas	Overseas investment in the UK
	Direct	Direct		Direct	Direct
1963	-315	257	1978	-3,520	1,962
1964	-397	193	1979	-5,889	3,030
1965	-464	249	1980	-4,867	4,355
1966	-386	309	1981	-6,005	2,932
1967	-399	354	1982	-4,091	3,027
1968	-492	500	1983	-5,417	3,386
1969	-649	446	1984	-6,036	-181
1970	-699	620	1985	-8,449	4,506
1971	-814	729	1986	-11,678	5,837
1972	-808	482	1987	-19,239	9,449
1973	-2,040	1,111	1988	-20,944	12,006
1974	-1,878	1,881	1989	-21,515	18,567
1975	-1,326	1,518	1990	-9,553	18,634
1976	-2,419	1,653	1991	-10,261	12,045
1977	-2,399	2,546			

Table 7.3 Multinational investment into the UK and overseas, 1963–1991

Until 1989 the UK was a net direct overseas investor, however in recent years this trend seems to have been reversed. This suggests that the UK is a popular European investment location and that in particular, prior to 1989, direct foreign investment was widely practised by UK businesses.

7.6 Why do firms go multinational?

Many of the advantages that MNC's gain are as a result of the fact that they are big business. However we can identify a number of advantages that are particular to the MNC. These might include:

☐ **spreading risk**. MNC's can spread their business operations over many markets. They are therefore less vulnerable to the fluctuations that might occur within any single economy.

☐ **competitive advantages**. A large foreign MNC may have a number of distinct economic advantages over domestic producers for example; economies of scale; management skills; technology. By using such advantages the MNC can easily capture a share of the market from existing producers.

☐ **lower labour** and **other resource costs**. The MNC can exploit differences in the price of resources between country's, thereby helping it to maximise its profits.

☐ **lower transport costs**. MNC's might locate their operations overseas to reduce the cost of transporting goods between markets.

☐ **avoiding trade barriers**. Many countries erect tariff (tax) barriers or use quotas in order to limit import trade. As a consequence businesses are forced to locate behind such barriers if they wish to continue to sell without restriction in such markets.

☐ **exploiting differences in government policy**. Many governments actively encourage MNC's to invest in their country. They offer a whole range of financial and other incentives and reduce many of the fixed or sunk costs that such companies would have to meet. This reduces much of the risk such investment might carry.

Activity

What problems might a business face if it decided to go multinational?

If a business decided to go multinational it might face some or all of the following problems; language barriers; communication and co-ordination problems between subsidiaries; selling and marketing in a foreign market with social and cultural differences; a lack of knowledge of foreign law and legal requirements.

7.7 The effects of multinational investment on the economy

As mentioned above many governments actively encourage MNC to locate in their countries. What benefits is multinational investment likely to bring? The benefits of multinational investment are argued to be:

☐ **employment**. Many MNC's are encouraged to locate in the more depressed regions of the host economy. It is in these areas that they are likely to attract more significant government aid. The employment that such companies create is both directly in the form of workers in the new production facility, and indirectly through the impact this will have on the local economy.

❑ **the balance of payments**. The balance of payments will benefit from both an inflow of capital and the use of the new production facility as an export platform.

❑ **technology transfer**. Many MNC's bring with them new technology. Many host nations might not have had access to such technology. If workers are also trained in its use then this might also be seen as some transferred advantage from the MNC.

❑ **living standards**. Many MNC's pay high wages, this will improve the living standards of those who are employed and the welfare of the country as a whole.

Activity

Multinational investment is not always seen as beneficial. What disadvantages or costs might such investment create?

The following problems of multinational investment might be identified:

❑ **competition** and **unemployment**. An MNC will have a highly competitive business operation that uses the most up-to-date technology and working practices, this may result in domestic producers being driven out of business. The subsequent loss in employment may well offset the gains made from the initial arrival of the MNC.

❑ **repatriation of profits**. All the profits made by the MNC may simply return to the company's home country.

❑ **uncertainty**. MNC's are 'foot loose' meaning that they can simply close down their operations in foreign countries and move. A country that has a large multinational sector within the economy will become very vulnerable to such activity.

❑ **control**. MNC's can, in particular circumstances, exert significant power and influence over national governments. This is particularly so in many developing countries where MNC's are not only the major employers but in many cases the principle wealth creators.

❑ **the environment**. MNC's may invest in countries simply to gain access to natural resources, which may be extracted or used in a way that is not sensitive to the environment.

Summary

Both small firms and multinationals play a significant role in the performance of the economy. While small firms can exploit their flexibility in dealing with ever changing market conditions, multinationals can exploit the potentials from having subsidiaries and outlets spread around the world.

Further reading

Dunnett A., *Understanding the Market*, Longman, 1992, Chapter 11.

Progress questions

1. Three criteria that might distinguish a small business are: ....
....

2. Small businesses are more flexible than big businesses.   True ☐   False ☐

3. Small businesses find it easy to expand.   True ☐   False ☐

4. Three ways in which the government could assist the small business sector would
be: ....
....

5. A multinational can be defined as a company that: ....
....

6. Firms go multinational so as to spread risk.   True ☐   False ☐

7. Governments might encourage multinational investment because: ....
....

8. Five reasons why multinational investment might not be beneficial to a country
are: ....
....

Review questions

11. What difficulties are there in defining the small business sector? (Section 7.2)

12. Outline the principle advantages the small business sector might have over the big
business sector.(Section 7.3)

13. Outline the principle advantages the big business sector might have over the small
business sector.(Section 7.6)

Multiple choice questions

14. Which of the following is **not** an advantage of a small firm:
    (a) low overhead costs.
    (b) flexibility in the face of change.
    (c) access to finance.
    (d) operate in niche markets and sell specialist products.

15. Which of the following is **not** an advantage of being a multinational:

    (a) risks can be spread.

    (b) market imperfections can be exploited.

    (c) trade barriers can be avoided.

    (d) business activities are easily co-ordinated on a global scale.

Practice questions

16. 'Without government assistance small firms would find it difficult to grow.' Assess this statement.

17. Outline the costs and benefits of having large scale multinational investment within the economy?

Assignment

Arrange an interview with the owner/manager of a local small business. Gather information on the following points:

What advantages are there in running a small business?

What economic problems do they face?

How might government help the business to be more successful?

As part of this exercise you might attempt to devise a questionnaire, and conduct your own local survey of small business and its problems.

8   The labour market and the determination of wages

8.1   Introduction

In this chapter we will focus upon the market for labour. Since the early 1980's the labour market has undergone great change, not only affecting the working lives of many workers, but also leading to a radical change in how many business's organise productive.

On completing this chapter you should be able to:

❐ describe the key characteristics and recent changes in the UK labour market;

❐ define the terms "demand" and "supply" of labour;

❐ show how wages are determined in a competitive labour market;

❐ describe the impact of trade unions on wage determination;

❐ define what is meant by collective bargaining;

❐ list a number of recent changes in labour market legislation;

❐ describe the impact Japanese working practices have had on the UK labour market.

8.2   The UK labour market

Changes in the structure of the labour market are a good indicator of wider changes being experienced by the economy. Table 8.1 shows the changes in labour market structure between 1978 and 1990.

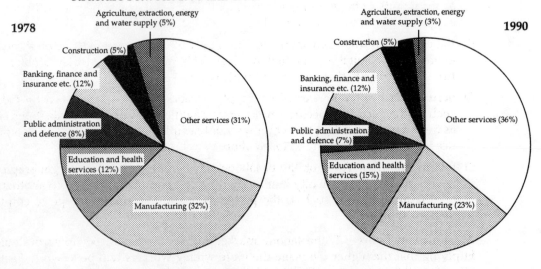

Table 8.1 Changes in labour market structure, 1978 and 1990

Activity

Using the data above outline the main changes in labour market structure. What might this suggest about the structure of the UK economy in general?

The two most important trends are:

❏ the rise in service sector employment;

❏ the decline in manufacturing employment.

What this suggests about the economy is that it is moving away from being a manufacturer to being a service provider. The UK economy is experiencing a phenomenon known as **deindustrialisation**. This will have a significant impact upon the skills required of the work force.

8.3 The determination of wages in a competitive market

In order to analyse how wages are determined in a competitive labour market we must first consider what factors determine both the supply and demand for labour.

The **supply of labour** is determined by the following factors:

❏ the **wage rate**. The wage rate is specific to any given industry or firm and thus influences the labour that it can attract.

❏ **demographic conditions**. The overall size of the labour force, which will be influenced by factors such as the birth and death rates and also the flow of migrants both into and out of the country, will determine the number of workers available for employment.

❏ **non-wage benefits**. If particular types of employment have beneficial perks, such as the quality of the working environment or long holidays, this may influence the supply of labour into such a market.

❏ the **number of qualified workers**. The supply of labour may be affected if there is a shortage of suitably qualified workers. This may be a particular problem for firms or industries that operate in highly specialised markets.

❏ **occupational entry barriers**. The supply of labour will be influenced by factors such as the need for specific employment qualifications or by organizations such as trade unions insisting that employers only employ union members. Such a practice is known as operating a **closed shop**.

❏ **labour mobility**. The mobility of labour may be influenced by both **geographical** factors such as the difficulty in moving from one part of the country to another, or **occupational** factors, such as the problems in shifting from one type of employment to another.

As shown in figure 8.1, the labour market supply curve will be upward sloping, implying that the higher the wage the more willing workers will be to work. Factors other than the wage level will determine where the labour supply curve is positioned.

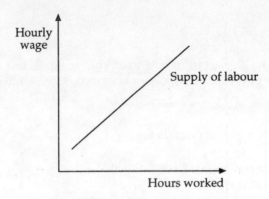

Figure 8.1 A labour supply curve

The **demand for labour** in a competitive labour market is assumed to be determined by the **marginal revenue product of labour (MRP$_L$)**. The MRP$_L$ refers to the extra earning or revenue gained from employing one more worker. This is simply found by multiplying what the worker produces by the price at which the output is sold. Table 8.2 below shows the MRP from employing additional units of labour. Due to the **law of diminishing returns**, as more labour is added to a given stock of machinery the physical product of what the worker produces begins to fall. As a consequence the additional revenue earned by each additional worker will also fall.

Number of workers	Total physical product (TTP)	Marginal physical product (MPP)	Price (P)	Marginal revenue product (MRP)
0	0			
		100	3	300
1	100			
		60	3	180
2	160			
		50	3	150
3	210			
		30	3	90
4	240			
		20	3	60
5	260			
		10	3	30
6	270			

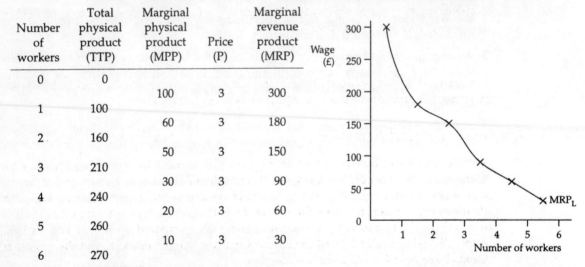

Table 8.2 Calculating the marginal revenue product of labour

Figure 8.2 The marginal revenue product of labour curve

The MRP curve (see Figure 8.2) represents the firms demand for labour. It shows how many workers would be employed at any given wage rate.

In a competitive environment we would assume that a profit maximising firm would employ labour up to the point where the marginal cost of labour (MC$_L$) is equal to the marginal revenue product of labour (MRP$_L$). The MC$_L$ in a competitive market will be the market determined wage, over which the individual firm has no control.

For example in figure 8.3 we can see that the quantity of labour employed given a wage of £115 will be three. At this point MC$_L$ = MRP$_L$.

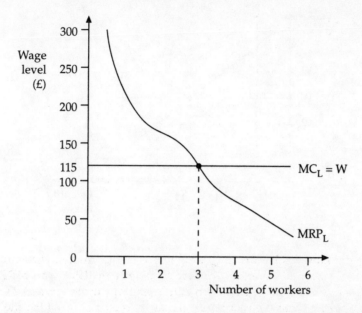

Figure 8.3 Wage determination in a competitive market

Activity

Considering figure 8.3 which area represents the total wage cost to the employer and which area represents profit?

The area below the wage level and up to 3 workers represents the wage bill to the business, the area above this is the profit made by the employer.

8.4 Trade unions and wage determination

A trade union can be defined as an organization formed to protect and further the interests of the worker. Such organizations originated from the craft guilds set up during the middle ages. However, they only became a common feature of industrial life for many workers towards the end of the 19th century. It is estimated that by 1920 over 45% of the labour force were union members, compared with only 11% in 1892. In the UK today under 40% of the labour force are union members, and the largest 10 unions have over 60% of all union members.

The existence of a trade union may have a significant impact upon the process of wage determination. Unions may influence both the supply of labour and through **collective bargaining**, directly influence the wage level. In either case the trade union may be forced to make a trade-off between employment and wage goals. In Figure 8.4 we can identify the competitive market wage and level of employment as W_1 Q_{L1}. If wages were forced upwards towards W_2 then the quantity of labour employed, assuming that the MRP curve remains constant, would fall. Only if the productivity of labour rises could this be avoided. Equally if a union seeks to increase the level of employment to Q_{L3} then the wage will fall to W_3.

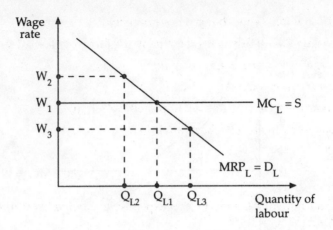

Figure 8.4 The determination of wages and trade unions

Activity

What factors might influence the wage the union asks for and the wage employers are willing to pay?

The following factors might be identified as important elements in the process of collective bargaining:

☐ **union power**. The stronger a trade union the more likely it will be able to force employers, through threats such as strike action, to give in to its wage demands.

☐ **profits**. This will influence the firms ability to award wage increases.

☐ **productivity**. Agreements to improve productivity and improve efficiency will mean that the MRP_L will rise, employers will then be able to award higher wage increases.

☐ the **cost of living**. Rising inflation will give rise to demands for larger pay increases as workers attempt to avoid a fall in their living standards.

☐ **comparability**. The wage level negotiated in one industry may frequently come to shape wage level demands throughout the economy, as workers look to maintain parity with other groups of workers.

☐ **unemployment**. A depressed labour market that has a surplus of labour will influence wage demands. It would signal to workers that the economy was likely to be in recession and hence employment was less secure. Unions would as a consequence moderate their demands.

8.5   The labour market and legislation

Changes in labour market legislation since 1979 have had a significant impact upon industrial relations in the UK. The main focus of such legislation has been in reducing the power and influence of trade unions over working practices and wage determination. Further measures have attempted to remove other labour market restrictions such as the fixing of minimum wages by government run **wages councils**.

Since 1979 the following changes have occurred:

❑ unions are now liable to legal action in the face of unlawful industrial action;

❑ secondary picketing is now illegal;

❑ strikes are now subject to a secret ballot;

❑ union leaders are now subject to periodic election;

❑ the wages councils have been abolished.

Activity

What economic impacts might you expect such changes in labour market legislation to lead to?

You might have considered the following:

❑ fewer strikes and other forms of industrial action. Strike action and the number of days lost through strike action have declined greatly since the strike prone 1970's. Legislation has had a large impact upon the incidence of strike activity, however other factors such as high unemployment would also have had a significant effect.

❑ a lower general level of wage increases. Wage increases fell sharply in the early 1980's and have been relatively constant since, standing at about 6% per annum. Reduced union power may have contributed to this, however as listed in the activity to section 8.4, other factors may also influence the determination of wages.

❑ lower rates of pay for certain groups of workers. Research findings have suggested that many workers who's wages were set by the wages council have seen their wages fall with the councils abolition.

❑ higher labour productivity. The reduced influence of trade unions has enabled many employers to more freely introduce new technology into the work process, and embrace many new working practices. This has helped contribute to a large rise in labour productivity throughout the 1980's.

8.6   The Japanization of British working practices

Many of the new working practices employed by British business, during the 1980's, have been largely adopted from the practices of Japanese business. Much of the success of the Japanese economy since 1945 has been put down to its superior way of running its work organisations. Such working practices have involved:

❑ a commitment to continuously **improving quality**. The use of **Total Quality Management (TQM)** is the title given to this strategy and involves all employees looking to improve the quality of the firms product.

❑ a commitment to **eliminate waste**. Japanese manufacturers use a technique known as **Just-In-Time (JIT)**. This involves insuring that only the necessary quantity of parts are delivered at the right time and place. JIT will aim to carry no stock, and is as such a highly efficient form of production organisation.

❏ the desire to achieve the total **flexibility** of the labour force. This involves flexibility in respect to what the worker does (**functional flexibility**), and also whether they are employed upon a permanent or temporary basis (**numerical flexibility**).

❏ a belief that **team working** is a superior form of work organization. Japanese companies encourage working team meetings as forums to help improve quality and discuss performance issues.

British manufacturers in the face of stiff foreign competition, have sought to adopt many of these working practices. This has in part only been possible due to the significant changes in labour market legislation since 1979.

Activity

In what ways might functional and numerical flexibility be of value to a manager running a business organization?

Functional flexibility would enable managers to move labour between various tasks and activities. Such workers would be multi-skilled and could undertake a wide range of responsibilities. A workforce that is numerically flexible would be advantageous as managers could easily hire and fire workers depending upon the level of demand for the businesses product or service. Hence the business would have far greater control over its labour costs.

Summary

In this chapter we have outlined some of the principle factors that influence both the demand and supply of labour and the determination of wages. We have assessed how such factors have changed with new legislation and the adoption of new labour practices. It is clear from our review of the labour market that it has changes greatly since the 1970's

Further reading

Sloman J, *Economics,* Harvester Wheatsheaf, (1994), Chapters 9 and 10 selectively.

Livesey F, *Economics,* Longman, (1989), Chapter 8.

Hare P and Simpson L, *British Economic Policy,* Harvester Wheatsheaf, (1993) Chapter 11.

Progress questions

1. Give two important ways the UK labour market has changed in recent years

    ....

2. A change in the wage rate will cause A MOVEMENT ALONG/A SHIFT IN the labour supply curve.

3. The marginal revenue product of labour refers to: ....

    ....

4. The marginal revenue product of labour is subject to DIMINISHING RETURNS/ ECONOMIES OF SCALE.

5. The process of collective bargaining is: ....
   ....

6. List six factors that might determine the outcome of the collective bargaining

   process: ....

   ....

7. If the marginal revenue product remains constant a rise in wages will likely cause employment to RISE/FALL.

8. List five ways in which labour market legislation has changed practices in the

   labour market: ....

   ....

9. Japanese working practices involve: ....

   ....

10. A numerically flexible workforce means there are always enough workers.

    True ☐ False ☐

Review questions

11. What factors will influence labour supply? (Section 8.3)

12. Explain how wages are determined in a competitive labour market. (Section 8.3)

13. Why must unions trade off higher employment with lower wages? Could this be avoided? (Section 8.4)

14. What impact have changes in labour market legislation had upon the labour market? Outline the advantages and disadvantages. (Section 8.5)

15. What is superior about Japanese working practices? (Section 8.6)

Multiple choice questions

16. Which of the following will **not** cause the supply of a particular type of skilled labour to shift right.
    (a) An increase in the number of qualified workers.
    (b) The government offers workers generous work relocation grants.
    (c) A substantial rise in the wage rate.
    (d) Union negotiators manage to win a wide range of non-wage benefits such as longer holidays.

17. A profit maximising firm will employ workers up to the point where:

    (a) MRP_L is at a maximum

    (b) $MRP_L = MCL$

    (c) $MRP_L \times P = W$

    (d) Diminishing returns set in.

18. Which of the following is not seen as a key feature of Japanese working practices:

    (a) Maintaining high levels of stock.

    (b) Continually improving product quality.

    (c) Reducing the role of the division of labour.

    (d) Ensuring the maximum level of flexibility from the work force.

Practice questions

19. Explain how productivity agreements made between employers and their workers may influence the level of wage settlement.

20. Assess the advantages and disadvantages of a labour market that is free from union involvement.

21. In what ways might Japanese working practices influence the process and level of wage settlement?

Assignment

Using various statistical sources find out how the average earnings for a range of alternative types of occupation have change over a 10 year period. How far can marginal productivity theory explain, (i) the difference in wage levels between occupational groups, and (ii) the difference in wage levels experienced over time. Statistical sources you might consider are The New Earnings Survey, The Annual Abstract of Statistics and Economic Trends.

9 Investment, R & D and training

9.1 Introduction

In order for an economy to remain competitive in world markets it must constantly update its level of technology. Failure to do so will condemn the economy to inevitable stagnation and decline. Investment is the key to creating such a dynamic economic system.

On completing this chapter you should be able to:

❒ define the term "investment";

❒ outline the main factors that determine the level of investment;

❒ show how business can appraise alternative investment projects;

❒ identify alternative sources for investment finance;

❒ outline the importance of R&D for the economy;

❒ describe how training and economic performance are linked;

❒ outline the UK's approach to training programmes.

9.2 What is investment?

Investment can be defined as the process of adding to the stock of capital assets within the economy. Given this we can distinguish between investment and saving. The purchase of a new machine by a business would be a form of investment, whereas the purchase of a rare painting would be a form of saving.

As investment adds to the capital stock of an economy, total investment is referred to as **Gross Domestic Fixed Capital Formation (GDFCF)**. GDFCF is composed of both **replacement** investment and **induced**(new) investment. As such only induced investment is an addition to the capital stock, replacement investment merely reflects the depreciation of existing assets. Therefore in order to identify only the induced part of investment we must distinguish between **gross** investment and **net** investment. Net investment is gross investment minus replacement investment. It is net investment that is the key to a growing and prosperous economy.

| | Analysed by sector | | | | Analysed by type of asset | | | Total gross |
	Private sector	General government	Public corporation	Dwellings	Other new building and works	Vehicles ships and aircraft	Plant and machinery	domestic fixed capital formation
1986	67 877	9 163	6 645	20 170	27 510	8 493	27 512	83 685
1987	78 013	9 027	5 220	21 728	31 600	9 846	29 086	92 260
1988	92 043	7 579	5 104	24 809	35 775	10 372	33 770	104 726
1989	94 778	10 054	5 671	23 822	37 525	11 231	37 925	110 503
1990	89 162	12 659	4 955	20 757	38 991	10 266	36 762	106 776
1991	79 697	12 688	3 880	16 778	37 522	8 008	33 957	96 265
1992	76 552	13 765	4 424	17 403	37 154	7 306	32 878	94 741

Source: Economic Trends

	Germany	France	Italy	UK	EU12	USA	Japan
1986	18.5	19.3	19.7	16.8	19.0	19.1	27.3
1987	17.2	19.8	19.7	17.5	19.3	18.5	28.5
1988	17.5	20.7	20.1	19.1	20.0	18.3	29.9
1989	19.2	21.2	20.2	20.1	20.7	17.7	31.0
1990	19.4	21.2	20.2	19.3	20.9	16.8	32.2
1991	18.2	20.8	19.8	16.7	20.3	15.4	31.6
1992	17.5	20.0	19.4	15.6	19.8	15.4	31.1
1993	17.9	19.6	19.3	15.5	19.6	15.3	31.2

Source: The European Economy No54 1993
Table 9.1 UK investment by sector and asset and
GDFCF as a % of GDP for various countries

Activity

Using the data presented in Table 9.1 what does it suggest concerning the UK's investment performance since 1979?

GDFCF rose steadily from 1986 to 1989 reflecting the expansion of the British economy over this period. It then fell sharply as a consequence of rising interest rates and a fall in business confidence. Buildings, and plant and machinery, are the most significant forms of investment asset and the private sector provides the largest source of investment funds. Internationally Britain devotes a smaller percentage of its GDP to investment than its main economic rivals. Only the USA invests a similar percentage to that of the UK. Japan invests over 10 percentage points more of its GDP than its nearest rival. Such an attitude towards investment would give the Japanese economy a huge competitive advantage on world markets.

9.3   Factors that influence investment

The following factors may be identified as determining whether a business invests or not. These are:

❑ **the rate of interest**. The higher the cost of borrowing money, the lower will be the level of investment. Conversely, the lower the rate the more likely investment is to rise, as investment projects with lower rates of return now become profitable.

❑ the level of **current profits**. The more profitable a business the less money it will need to borrow for investment purposes, the more likely it is to invest more.

❑ **expectations of future profit**. The more confident the business is concerning the growth in its market the more likely it is to invest in order to meet such anticipated demand.

❑ the **cost and productivity of capital goods**. If capital goods become cheaper or more efficient then the return on any investment will rise, businesses will be encouraged to invest more.

❑ **access to finance**. The more willing banks are to provide funds for business investment the more likely business may be in investing. A banking sector that is not prepared to risk money may impose restrictions on business lending so discouraging investment.

Activity

How might government influence the level of investment within the economy?

Government can influence the level of investment within the economy directly and indirectly. Directly it can offer investment grants or other incentives which reduce the costs of investment, such as providing facilities like new buildings. Indirectly government can attempt to shape business expectations through its management of the economy, stimulate the level of consumer demand, or through its tax policy, shift the tax burden from company profits. All of these measures might contribute to a stimulus of investment.

9.4 Investment appraisal

Once a business has decided that it wishes to invest it must then reach a decision concerning which investment project(s) to pursue. The choice of investment project will largely be determined by its profitability. In order for a business to make a rational informed decision between such projects they must attempt to calculate the profitability that such alternative investment will yield. The difficulty lies in the fact investment projects yield profits over a given period of time. It is the prediction of such **cash flows** that creates uncertainty.

We can identify three techniques that businesses might employ in order to aid their assessment and selection of alternative investment projects. These are:

❑ **The payback method**. Using such an approach investment projects are assessed upon how long it would take for revenue from the investment to repay the projects initial cost. Therefore a project that yields a faster flow of funds, such as repaying the initial investment in four years, would be perceived as superior to projects that might take longer. The problem with such a method is that it fails to consider revenue flows over the longer term. Slow yielding projects might, given a longer time horizon, prove to be more profitable.

❑ **The net present value method (NPV)**. In order to compare investment projects that might yield cash flows at varying rates and so distort the possible superiority of one project over another, we must conduct a process of **discounting**. That is reducing or discounting expected future cash flows back to present values. Whether a project is accepted or rejected will greatly depend on the **rate of discount** that we select to use.

The NPV technique attempts to assess whether an investment project yields, over its lifetime, a surplus of funds greater than the projects initial outlay costs, given the cost of capital required for funding. If the NPV is positive then the project is deemed profitable, otherwise the project should be rejected. The formula for calculating the NPV is given as:

$$NPV = \frac{(R-C)}{(1+k)} + \frac{(R-C)_2}{(1+k)^2} + \frac{(R-C)_3}{(1+k)^3} + \dots \frac{(R-C)_n}{(1+k)^n} - C_0$$

where R is the projects yearly earnings, C is the yearly cost, $(1-k)$ is the discount rate which is expressed as a fraction, C_0 represents the initial outlay of the project.

An example. Let us assume that a £7000 machine (C_0) will generate £2000 for five years ($R - C$) and then go for scrap anticipated to fetch a further £500. The cost of finance is 10%, hence our discount rate k is 0.1. Is this investment project worthwhile?

Summing together the present values we have:

$$\text{NPV} = \underset{\text{Year 1}}{\frac{2000}{1.1}} + \underset{\text{Year 2}}{\frac{2000}{1.21}} + \underset{\text{Year 3}}{\frac{2000}{1.33}} + \underset{\text{Year 4}}{\frac{2000}{1.46}} + \underset{\text{Year 5}}{\frac{2500}{1.61}} - £7000$$

$$= £1818 + £1653 + £1503 + £1370 + £1553 - £7000$$

$$= £7897 - £7000$$

$$= £897$$

The investment project generates a profit of £897 and can thus be seen as worthwhile.

❑ **The internal rate of return method (IRR)**. This technique for assessing whether an investment is worthwhile involves finding at what rate of discount a project would breakeven. This rate is then compared to the current discount rate, if this is less than the breakeven discount rate the project should proceed as the rate of return is greater than would be achieved from leaving the money in the bank.

Activity

Using the example above calculate the NPV if the rate of discount increased from 10% to 15%. Is the project now worthwhile?

A 5% increase in the discount rate reduces the present value to £6957. The project is no longer profitable and should be rejected.

9.5 Financing investment

Given the importance of the cost of capital and hence the discount rate in determining whether an investment project is worth pursuing, the factors affecting the cost of finance are crucial in our assessment of investment appraisal.

Business can finance investment by either:

❑ **borrowing**;

❑ **retaining profits**;

❑ **issuing new shares**.

Table 9.2 shows the sources of finance used for investment purposes by UK business.

| Internal Funds | | External Borrowing | | | | | | | | | |
Total	%	Total	%	Bank	%	Share	%	Overseas	%	Other	%
1988	40,085	(40)	57,766	(58)	38,393	(38)	11,481	(12)	7,892	(8)	2,023	(2)
1989	35,727	(33	70,959	(66)	44,108	(41)	15,892	(15)	10,959	(10)	1,339	(1)
1990	30,287	(35	53,779	(63)	28,036	(33)	14,027	(16)	11,716	(14)	1,796	(2)
1991	34,904	(50	33,967	(48)	3,335	(5)	21,446	(30)	9,186	(13)	1,229	(2)
1992	34,251	(62)	19,836	(36)	–660	(–1)	14,604	(26)	5,892	(11)	1,005	(2)

Source: Economic Trends
Table 9.1 Sources of investment funds

Up until 1987 the overwhelming source of investment capital came from ploughed back profits or **internal** funds. **External** finance such as borrowing from banks became more prevalent towards the end of the 1980's. It is quite common that an individual business will in fact raise capital from a range of sources. Hence calculating the cost of capital for investment purposes, comprised as it may be of a mixture of bank and share or equity finance, means that we must consider the businesses **gearing ratio**. The gearing ratio refers to the proportion of debt to equity finance held by a business. It is traditionally assumed that the cost of capital is simply an average of the cost of debt and the cost of equity. As such a change in the businesses gearing ratio will influence the cost of capital and hence the businesses investment decision.

Activity

Why will the cost of capital rise at a growing rate as the gearing ratio rises, such as illustrated in Figure 9.1?

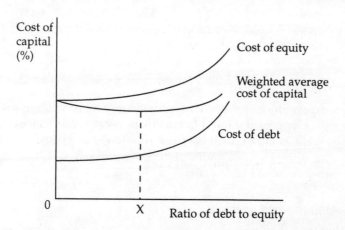

Figure 9.1 The cost of capital

It is assumed that shareholders will allow a firm to finance investment from bank borrowing as compared to equity since it is cheaper source of finance. The cost of capital will be minimised. However, at a certain point of gearing, the debt of the firm will make it a risky investment. Both shareholders and those who control the loans made to the firm will now demand a higher return on their finance to cover the risk of business failure. Hence the cost of capital will begin to rise steeply.

9.6 Research and Development

As well as the need for investment to help stimulate and constantly update the productive capacity of the economy, a vital component of a thriving economic system is the research and development of new products and processes. However, a high level of R&D does not automatically imply that we will see a significant improvement in economic performance. The reason for this is that we must distinguish between **invention**, **innovation** and the **diffusion** of innovations.

❑ Invention refers to a contribution to technology.

❑ Innovation refers to the commercialisation of the invention, that is its use within the productive process.

❑ Diffusion is where the invention has a wide spread influence upon the performance of the economy as a whole. It is only at this point that we can describe the outputs derived from R&D contributing in a positive way to the growth of the economy and our international competitive position.

Activity

Table 9.3 compares the level of R&D as a percentage of gross domestic product (GDP) for the major industrial economies. How has the UK economy performed over the late 1980's and early 1990's?

	UK	Germany	France	Italy	Japan	Canada	USA
1986	2.29	2.73	2.23	1.13	2.56	1.47	2.91
1987	2.22	2.88	2.27	1.19	2.63	1.42	2.87
1988	2.18	2.86	2.28	1.22	2.67	1.37	2.84
1989	2.20	2.87	2.33	1.24	2.80	1.36	2.80
1990	2.19	2.73	2.42	1.30	2.88	1.44	2.77
1991	2.08	2.58	2.42p	1.38p	2.86	1.46p	2.78

p = provisional

Table 9.3 International comparisons of R&D as a % of GDP, 1986–1991

General expenditure on research and development (GERD) in the UK has been significantly better than in Italy and Canada, and similar to France. The level of GDP allocated to R&D in Japan, Germany and the USA is approximately $\frac{1}{2}$% point higher in most years. This is a significant difference over the longer term as the cumulative level of resources devoted to R&D rises.

9.7 Training and economic performance

As well as the investment made by business into new plant and machinery, business is also a key investor in human resources. Education and training, which we might term **human capital**, is a vital component required for economic success. The two are linked in the following ways:

❑ a new wave of technology will only have a significant impact upon the economy if the workforce is suitably skilled;

❑ the expansion of business is limited by the quantity of skilled workers. A skills shortage will tend to push up wages and cause production costs to rise;

❑ a poorly trained workforce will be less productive and hence more inefficient than one that is well trained;

❑ a more skilled workforce will offer the business greater flexibility in responding to market fluctuations (see section 8.6).

Training in the UK was, up until the establishment of the Training Boards in 1964, the total responsibility of the employers. As a consequence it was found that the level of training within the economy was highly sensitive to fluctuations in the business cycle. In times of recession employers were prone to cut back on investment and in particular investment in training. By the early 1970's Britain was facing a persistent skills shortage. The government responded by assuming more responsibility for maintaining training levels. It established the **Manpower Service Commission (MSC)** in 1973 which was an attempt to co-ordinater training initiatives between both the public and private sectors.

Since 1979 there have been many changes in government training policies. The most significant of which are listed in Table 9.4 below.

Initiative	Description
Post-16 education and training	
Youth Training Scheme (1983)	Provides two years of work-related training including at least 13 weeks off-the-job training or relevant further education, for 16-year-old school-leavers, and one year of training for 17-year-olds. Participants receive placement guarantee and maintenance allowance.
Certificate of Pre-Vocational Education (1985)	Aimed at young people who wish to continue in full-time education after the age of 16 to prepare for either work or vocational courses. Included a period of work experience.
Technical and Vocational Education Initiative (1987)	Provides a mixed general and vocational education for 14- to 18-year-olds. Participants take available vocational and academic qualifications.
Advanced Supplementary Exams (1987)	Equivalent to one half of an A-Level, in terms of content. Aims to broaden the range of post-16 study.
Training Credits Scheme (1991)	Provides young people with an entitlement to purchase training from employers or training centres.
National Vocational Qualifications (1992)	Aims to implement a comprehensive system of vocational qualifications based on four levels of achievement.
Advanced Diploma	Awarded for satisfactory performance in A Levels, or in level 3 NVQs, or in a mixture of the two. Aims to create parity of prestige between vocational and academic education.
Higher Education	
Education Reform Act (1988)	Introduction of competitive bidding among universities for student places. Aims to increase number of student places by lowering unit costs.
Top-up Loans (1989)	

Source: Oxford Review of Economic Policy Vol 8 No2
Table 9.4 Initiatives in education and training

As well as the development of these new training initiatives, the government also shifted the administration of training responsibility back to the private sector. The establishment of the **Training and Enterprise Councils (TEC's)** was seen to be a more effective way to deliver training at a local business community level. Such councils are run by local business leaders, who it is argued, are in a better position to know the skills requirements of local business. The role of government, given the TEC's, is now one of simply providing finance.

Activity

Comparative figures regarding the numbers trained and the level of qualification are shown in table 9.5. How does the UK compare internationally on the issue of training?

Numbers qualifying in engineering and technology, 1985

Per 100,000 population	UK	France	W. Germany	Japan
Doctorates	1.2	0.5	1.6	0.5
Master & enhanced degrees	4.0	11.0	7.0	8.0
Bachelor degrees	25.0	27.0	34.0	50.0
Technicians	51.0	63.0	72.0	46.0
Craftsmen	62.0	167.0	197.0	75.0

Source: NIESR

Table 9.5 Education and training comparisons

Where UK training appears to lag most significantly behind its main rivals is in the quantity of craftsman. The numbers achieving higher level qualifications are less of a problem. The figures tell us nothing about the quality of training. In order to assess this we would need to consider the length of training and also investigate the contribution of labour to business productivity.

Summary

We have shown in this chapter that investment is vital for creating a successful economy. Without investment economic growth will stagnate and a widening technological gap will appear between a country and it's major rivals. We have also shown that two further components are necessary if investment is to have its full impact upon the economy, there must be R&D and an adequately skilled workforce to expand with production.

Further reading

Livesey F, *Economics*, Longman, (1989), Chapter 16.

Beg D, *Economics* MaGraw Hill, (1994), Chapter 12.

Progress questions

1. Investment can be defined as: ....

....

2. Net investment is gross investment minus replacement investment.

   True ☐ False ☐

3. Five factors that will influence investment are: ....

   ....

4. An investment projects cash flow is: ....

5. The payback method of investment appraisal does not take account of slow profit yielding projects.

   True ☐ False ☐

6. The rate of discount is: ....

   ....

7. Three forms of investment finance are: ....

   ....

8. A firms gearing ratio is the ratio of internal to external finance.

   True ☐ False ☐

9. Without innovation, inventions will yield few if any profits.

   True ☐ False ☐

10. Four ways that training and economic performance are linked are: ....

    ....

Review questions

11. Investment is largely determined by the position of the economy in the trade cycle. Is this true? (Section 9.3)

12. Outline the different ways a business might appraise alternative investment projects. (Section 9.4)

13. What advantages are there in financing investment from internal funds. (Section 9.5)

14. Explain why a business might find it difficult to calculate the rate of discount. (Section 9.5)

15. Why are R&D and training so important to the future performance of the economy? (Sections 9.6 and 9.7)

Multiple choice questions

16. Which of the following will **not** cause the level of investment to rise.
    (a) The rate of interest falls.
    (b) The rate of economic growth within the economy improves.
    (c) A significant breakthrough in manufacturing technology.
    (d) Shareholders demand higher share dividends.

17. A businesses gearing ratio refers to:
    (a) the proportion of debt to equity finance held by the business.
    (b) the division of profits between investment and share dividends.
    (c) the ratio of capital to labour in the productive process.
    (d) the speed at which the business can grow.

18. During an economic recession the level of training is most likely to be:
    (a) low.
    (b) rising.
    (c) difficult to determine.
    (d) all of the above.

Practice question

19. 'Without continual investment the economy would stagnate.' Explain the rationale behind this statement.

20. Outline the advantages and disadvantages of leaving the level and quality of training to the free market.

21. How are the different market structures, as analysed in Chapter 6, likely to perform in respect to the level of investment, and also the quantity of R&D and training.

Assignment

One of the principle determinants of the level of investment within the economy is the state of business confidence. What factors shape business confidence? In this assignment you are to attempt to devise a means of measuring such confidence, such that you can estimate whether confidence is growing or falling and by how much. In order to achieve this you will not only be required to identify the criteria that shape business confidence, but also assess how important each factor is relative to other factors. Devise a questionnaire to be given to local business, and from this attempt to solve the problem outlined above.

10 National economic change and business activity

10.1 Introduction

This chapter introduces the student to the concept of economic growth and how such growth is subject to change. It highlights those factors that influence growth and identifies some of the difficulties facing government in attempting to manage the overall level of demand within the economy.

On completing this chapter you should be able to:

❑ distinguish between actual and potential growth and those factors that influence them;

❑ describe and illustrate how a simple model of the economy operates;

❑ define and apply the multiplier effect to particular courses of policy action;

❑ describe what is meant by the terms inflationary and deflationary gaps;

10.2 Economic growth

When considering economic growth it is important to distinguish between **actual growth** and **potential output**.

Actual growth is measured by what is actually produced over a given period, usually a year. Potential output is a measure of what the economy could produce given the efficient use of its available resources.

The major influence on the actual rate of growth within the economy is the level of **aggregate demand** (dealt with in 10.3). The potential output of the economy is determined by the availability of resources and the level of technology being used.

In the short-run a business may be concerned with and respond to changes in the actual growth rate within the economy. In the long-run the business needs to consider issues related to potential output, as these restrict the actual growth that the firm could achieve in the future; for example the need to invest in new machinery or new technology.

The growth in the economy is measured by the value of the nations output or, as it is termed in economics, its **gross domestic product (GDP)**. GDP can be calculated in three equivalent ways using:

❑ final expenditure on goods and services;

❑ the incomes generated from production;

❑ the value of everything produced.

GDP when added to income earned abroad is known as **gross national product (GNP)**. GNP figures may not state the full output of the nation as some goods and services may go unrecorded. The **underground economy** consists of illegal work that is not declared for tax purposes. The size of the underground economy is very difficult to calculate. In Italy it is estimated to be 15% of GDP, in the UK it is suggested to be a lot smaller, although no one is quite certain! Recent findings by the Inland Revenue estimate that the underground economy may be as large as £50bn.

Activity

In the previous chapter, section 9.3, we analysed the importance of investment for the economy. To recap on the key points consider what factors will influence the investment decision of a business? How might the chancellor of the exchequer set about influencing a business's level of investment in order to ensure the future expansion of the national economy?

A wide variety of factors may influence the investment decision of a business and hence its potential output in the future. The crucial ones that you might have identified, as explained in section 9.3, are:

☐ the level of demand and in particular whether it is rising or falling;

☐ the cost of borrowing;

☐ business expectations concerning the state of the economy;

☐ profitability and changes in technology.

Government economic policy can have both a direct and indirect effect upon the level of investment made. It can:

☐ manage the level of demand within the economy;

☐ attempt to shape business expectations by controlling fluctuations in economic activity;

☐ set interest rates;

☐ adjust the level of tax on money used for investment purposes;

☐ provide finance to firms in the form of grants and subsidies.

10.3 Economic growth and aggregate demand

Aggregate demand (AD) refers to the total level of spending within the economy. It consists of four elements:

consumer spending (C)

investment spending by firms (I)

government spending (G)

spending on our exports by foreigners (including their investment in the UK) (X)

To find the total level of spending in the economy we must subtract spending on imports (M) which represents a flow of spending abroad. AD can be shown as:

$$AD = C + I + G + (X - M)$$

If AD rises, businesses will respond by expanding production. Alternatively if AD falls businesses will cut back their level of output. Hence a rising level of AD is associated with an expanding or growing economy, whereas a falling level of demand is a characteristic of an economy with declining economic activity.

Actual growth tends to fluctuate from year to year. At certain points in time the economy may be experiencing a boom in economic activity. Alternatively the economy may be in decline and business activity in a slump. The economy tends to go through a cycle of such booms and slumps. In Figure 10.1 you can see the business cycle of the UK economy since 1950.

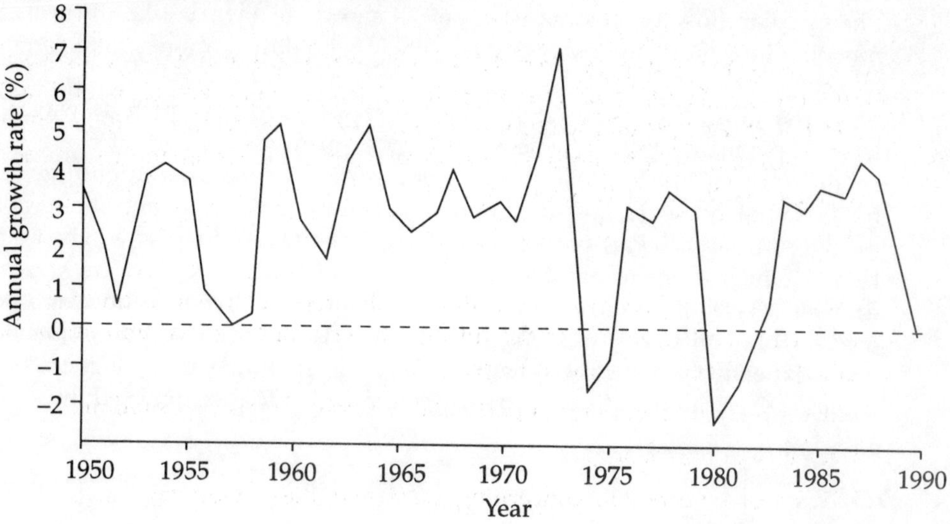

Source: Economic Trends
Figure 10.1 Economic growth in the UK since 1950

Although the length and intensity of the various phases of the cycle are unpredictable, the direction in which the economy is moving is very important in influencing the business decision-making process. For example, a business that observes a falling rate of economic growth or a steady decline in orders will be reluctant to invest in new machinery or hire additional workers. Such a decision will contribute to yet a further fall in business activity.

Activity

Whether the national economy is expanding or contracting will not only influence the level of growth within the economy, it also determines the performance of the other principal economic variables: unemployment, inflation and the balance of payments. How have each of these variables performed since 1986 when the UK first experienced a period of relative economic prosperity, followed by a period of relative stagnation from early 1990's?

In answering this question you should have first noted that in the case of a period of economic stagnation the level of demand within the economy is low, and in a period of prosperity, high. Therefore economic stagnation will be characterised by high unemployment, low inflation (the economy has spare capacity and prices are falling) and a balance of payments surplus (assuming that not only is demand for domestically produced goods low but also our demand for imported products will fall). In a period of prosperity, unemployment will be low, inflation high and the balance of payments in deficit. In between booms and slumps the variables of growth, unemployment, inflation and the balance of payments will be either rising or falling. It is such changes in these variables that governments are interested in identifying so that they might successfully intervene to control economic activity (see Chapter 12). In order to explain how governments might intervene in economic activity we must first devise a model concerning how the economy works.

10.4 Aggregate demand and the circular flow of income

The **circular flow of income** diagram as shown in Figure 10.2 illustrates a simple model of how the economy operates, showing the flow of money between households and consumers.

In the inner flow, households receive factor payments such as wages, rent and interest payments from businesses. They, in turn, spend part of these earnings on products produced by businesses. This represents **consumer spending** (C). Households do not, however, spend all of their earnings on the consumption of domestically produced products. Part of their earnings may be **saved** (S), part will be taken in **taxation** (T) and part spent on foreign **imports** (M). Both S, T and M are known as **withdrawals** (W) from the circular flow. Alternatively, not all money flowing into business comes from consumer spending. **Investment** (I) by banks or other financial institutions, expenditure by **government** (G) and the spending by foreigners on domestic **exports** (X) are all **injections** (J) or flows of money into the circular flow.

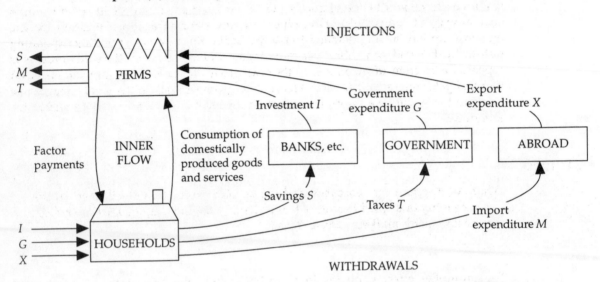

Figure 10.2 The circular flow of income

Subsequently the level of demand within the economy at any particular time depends upon the level of injections and/or withdrawals. If withdrawals are greater than injections, then there is a net outflow of money from the inner flow. Business will experience a falling level of demand for their products. By contrast, if injections are greater than withdrawals this will act as a stimulus upon the economy and business will experience a rising level of demand.

Activity

What would happen to the level of demand in the domestic economy if:

(i)   building societies and banks increase interest rates on savings accounts;

(ii) VAT is reduced to 10% from its current level of $17\frac{1}{2}$%;

(iii) business expectations are that the economy is on the verge of recession;

(iv) the pound falls in value against a number of competitors currencies;

(v) government decides to expand the existing motorway network.

In deciding upon the impact of the above on the level of demand you must first identify whether the effect is an injection or a withdrawal. An increase in interest rates on savings accounts will cause demand to fall as withdrawals increase, that is people save more. Alternatively, a cut in VAT will see a fall in withdrawals and hence a rise in demand. A fall in business expectations will cause investment to fall and hence a reduction in the overall level of injections. The final two questions will see injections and the level of demand rise. A fall in the pound means our exports become cheaper and an expansion of the motorway network will cause government spending to rise.

10.5 Aggregate demand and the multiplier effect

The **multiplier** refers to the effect that a given change in either the level of injections or withdrawals will have on the level of income. For example, if the government was to increase its level of spending the overall level of demand within the economy would be higher. Business organizations would respond by employing more resources in the production of goods and services and pay out more in factor incomes such as wages to households. Households in turn spend a fraction of this new income on consumption causing demand to rise yet again. Businesses respond by expanding output further and generating yet more income. However, each time this process is repeated a fraction of income is withdrawn from the inner flow, and the effect on demand gets smaller and smaller. Hence for a given rise(fall) in the level of aggregate demand there will be a multiplied effect on the level of economic activity within the economy.

Activity

What effect would the discovery and subsequent exploration of oil have on the local economy of a small fishing village? Identify the implications for local goods, service and factor markets such as labour.

The multiplier effect upon the local economy from the discovery and subsequent exploration of oil will create significant economic activity. Flows of money into the area will create new employment – both oil and non-oil related. The demand for local goods and services will rise. The arrival of migrant oil workers will lead to a demand for housing and other community services which will in turn stimulate the construction market and its related suppliers. This process will continue so long as the market expands.

10.6 Showing the multiplier effect

We can show the multiplier effect by constructing an injections and withdrawals diagram. This involves considering how injections and withdrawals change with the level of national income. When considering our three withdrawals we find that:

❏ as our income rises so will our level of saving;

❏ assuming that we have a progressive tax structure such that the more you earn the more tax you pay, then the level of tax paid will rise with income;

❏ the level of imports will also increase with rising income. Many imports are luxury goods which will be strongly influenced by high levels of income.

By contrast, injections are not determined by the level of national income, they are assumed constant at all level of income. Investment is determined by a wide range of factors including expectations, government spending is determined by government policy, and export earnings are determined by levels of national income in foreign countries.

When we plot our withdrawals and injections curve as in Figure 10.3 we can now identify the point at which the economy is in equilibrium (W=J).

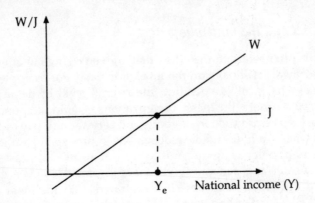

Figure 10.3 Injections and withdrawals in equilibrium

In order to now illustrate the multiplier effect (Figure 10.4) let us assume, as in our example above, that the government increases its overall level of spending within the economy. The injections curve would shift upwards to J_2 the level of national income will rise from Y_{e_1} to Y_{e_2}.

The multiplier is identified as the change in Y resulting from the change in J. Notice that the change in Y is a multiple of the initial change in J, this is the multiplier effect.

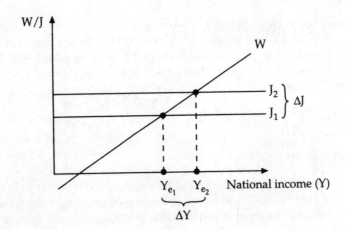

Figure 10.4 The multiplier effect

You should have shifted the curves in the following ways, (i) withdrawals shift up, (ii) withdrawals shift down, (iii) injections shift down, (iv) and (v) injections shift up.

10.7 Inflationary and deflationary gaps

It should now be apparent that the multiplier effect has important implications for governments who attempt to manage the level of demand within the economy. The economy at any one time is likely to experience either:

❏ an **inflationary gap**. That is one where the level of spending exceeds the level of output that can be produced hence causing prices to rise.

❏ a **deflationary gap**. That is one where the level of spending is less than the level of output being produced. Therefore resources are not being used to their full potential, for example labour is unemployed or machinery is not being run near full capacity.

If the economy is suffering from unemployment, that is experiencing a deflationary gap, then the government may find it desirable to stimulate demand to create more employment. It can do this by either raising injections or reducing withdrawals. In particular it can influence its own budget. The multiplier means however, that only a slight change in one of the components of aggregate demand may be necessary to remove the unemployment problem. Excess spending will simply over stimulate the economy, causing it to grow too quickly thus leading to inflationary pressure. Alternatively, if government attempts to reduce demand in an inflationary gap situation, excess cuts in the level of injections or increases in withdrawals may simply reduce economic activity such that businesses cut back on the level of production making resources, such as labour, redundant.

Using our withdrawals and injections curves we can illustrate such inflationary and deflationary positions (Figure 10.5a and 10.5b)

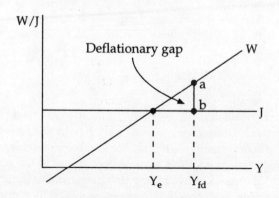

Figure 10.5a The deflationary gap

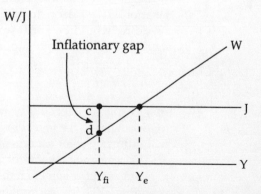

Figure 10.5b The inflationary gap

Let us assume that the economy is at a point such as Y_e in Figure 10.5a. In order to use all of society's resources and achieve **full employment**, the economy must expand income to Y_{fd}. The distance a-b represents this unused capacity and the deflationary gap. Likewise in Figure 10.5b, a point to the left of Y_e such as Y_{fi} which represents a full employment of resources, we can observe that the level of income and hence spending is too large and exceeds output, hence the distance c-d is an inflationary gap.

Activity

If the level of demand is to be changed in order to correct excessive unemployment or high rates of inflation, the government will want to adjust the level of AD by just the right amount. It is very important that government knows the size of the multiplier in order to achieve this end.

In calculating the multiplier we can use the following formula:

$k = 1/mpw$ where mpw $= \Delta W / \Delta Y$ (Δ = change in)

where the mpw is the marginal propensity to withdraw or the fraction of every pound that is not spent on consumption. Hence the larger the mpw the smaller will be the effect of a change in demand on the level of consumption of domestically produced goods.

(i)   Calculate the multiplier effect if the mpw is known to be a $\frac{1}{4}$.

(ii) If the economy was to experience an injection of £150m government spending what impact would this have on the level of income?

(iii) If a deflationary gap is known to be £4800 and the multiplier is 3, by how much should government increase its spending?

(iv) Which would have the greater effect on income, a rise in government spending or a cut in taxation?

The calculation of the multiplier is important as it will help determine the level of spending that is required in order to correct for the imbalances between consumption and output. The multiplier in (i) is 4. That is for every pound spent, £4 of income will be generated. Given this, if government spending increased by £150m, the impact upon the level of income would be 4 x £150m = £600m. As by way of another example concerning the importance of the multiplier. If there is a short fall in demand of £4800, and a known multiplier of 3, government would simply increase spending by £1600m. A rise in government spending would have a larger impact upon income than a cut in taxation. The reason for this is that all the money from a change in government spending would be spent, whereas a cut in tax may simply lead consumers to save more or consume more imports.

10.8 The accelerator effect

Any change in injections or withdrawals and the subsequent multiplier effect that will follow, will see the level of national income change. Such a change in national income will influence other aspects of the economy, in particular the level of investment.

The accelerator theory of investment relates the level of investment in the economy to changes in the level of national income. Let us assume that government increases its spending. Via the multiplier national income will rise. Investors will respond by investing more. Given that investment is an injection into the circular flow the impact on national income will be that it rises yet further. Another multiplier effect will take place. If the rate of increase in income is greater than in the previous time period, a further rise in investment can be expected. Investors will anticipate that present investment will be needed to satisfy future demand. If however the rate of increase in income is less than in the previous time period, investors will take this as a signal that the growth in the economy is slowing down. As they cut back on investment, injections into the circular flow will fall and the economy inevitably slows down.

The accelerator theory of investment suggests that the level of investment is determined by investor expectations. This means that it is very difficult to predict, due to the interaction between the multiplier and accelerator. The total effect upon the economy resulting from a given change in the level of national income is uncertain.

Activity

In order to illustrate the accelerator effect fill in the missing values in the table below. Assume that each machine used by the individual firm will produce 200 units of output and that 2 machines will need replacing each year.

What happens to investment between years 4 and 5 even given the fact that the level of demand has continued to rise?

Time period	0	1	2	3	4	5	6
Quantity demanded	1000	1000	2000	3000	5000	5400	5600
Number of machines required							
New investment							
Replacement investment							
Total investment							

Between years 4 and 5 even though the level of demand has continued to grow, it is now growing at a slower rate. As a result you should have found that investment falls from 12 to 4. The accelerator theory of investment argues that the level of investment is determined by the rate of growth in demand which is illustrated clearly by this point.

Summary

In this chapter we have considered how the macro economy works and how intervention by government can help the economy to function more effectively. We have identified the key concepts of the multiplier and accelerator and the economic implications of having an economy in a deflationary or inflationary economic position.

Further reading

Sloman J, *Economics*, Harvester Wheatsheaf, (1994), Chapters 13 –16.

Progress questions

1. Actual growth is determined by aggregate demand.   True ☐ False ☐

2. Potential growth is determined by the size of the labour force.   True ☐ False ☐

3. GDP measures: ....

4. Aggregate demand consists of: ....

5. The trade cycle shows: ....

6. The size of the multiplier is determined by the level of consumption.

   True ☐ False ☐

7. The relationship between withdrawals and income is a direct relationship.

   True ☐ False ☐

8. The multiplier can be defined as: ....

   ....

9. An INFLATIONARY/DEFLATIONARY gap is one where the level of spending exceeds the level of output.

10. The accelerator theory of investment suggests that investment is determined by the RATE OF INTEREST/EXPECTATIONS.

Review questions

11. How are the principle economic variables within the economy linked to the trade cycle?(Section 10.3)

12. Sketch the circular flow of income and explain its operation. (Section 10.4)

13. What is the multiplier effect and how is it calculated? (Section 10.6)

14. Distinguish between an inflationary and deflationary gap and explain how government might close such a gap. (Section 10.7)

15. Explain how the accelerator theory of investment works. (Section 10.8)

Multiple choice questions

16. The major determinant of potential output within an economy is:
    (a) aggregate demand.
    (b) the size of the underground economy.
    (c) available resources.
    (d) the level of competition in the market place.

17. If the government decided to increase government spending by £500m, what would be the final level of income created given a marginal propensity to consume (MPC) of 0.4. Would it be:
    (a) £830m
    (b) £200m
    (c) £900m
    (d) more information is required.

18. The accelerator effect is:
    (a) the speed at which policy will have an effect upon the economy.
    (b) the relationship between interest rates and the level of investment.
    (c) the relationship between business expectations and the level of investment.
    (d) the relationship between investment and the multiplier effect.

Practice questions

19. As the economy nears full employment explain why inflation is likely. What might government do in order to avoid such inflationary pressures?

20. Why might the size of the multiplier be difficult to calculate? What are the implications for government economic policy?

21. Assess what implications the material in Chapter 10 might have for the performance of business within the economy.

Assignment

Gather data concerning economic growth for the major European economies since 1979. Plot this data against time and see whether all the economies you have identified follow a similar cyclical growth path. What factors might lead you to expect that such economies will be closely linked? How might we account for differences in economic growth performance? Suitable reference sources might include The European Economy, various Economist Country Reports, and a wide range of OECD data publications.

11 *Money, banking and inflation*

11.1 *Introduction*

In this chapter we will focus upon the role of money within the economy. We will describe what money is, and consider the main functions of the various financial intermediaries that deal with it.

On completing this chapter you should be able to:

❏ list the main functions of money;

❏ distinguish between narrow and broad definitions of money;

❏ identify the main financial intermediaries and describe their role in the financial system;

❏ distinguish between a capital market and a money market;

❏ describe the process of credit creation;

❏ define what is meant by the term inflation and list its main causes;

❏ make an argument both for and against the adoption of an independent central bank.

11.2 *The functions of money*

Money performs four main functions, these are:

❏ **a medium of exchange**. In this sense money acts as the common means of payment for goods and services.

❏ **a means of storing value**. Money represents a form of asset in which individuals can store their wealth.

❏ **a unit of account**. Money can be used to value the worth of different goods and services.

❏ **a standard of deferred payment**. Money can be used as a convenient means of agreeing future payments for goods and services.

> *Activity*
>
> If a given commodity is to serve as money, what attributes would such a commodity need in order to function as a successful form of currency?

An ideal form of money might have the following characteristics; it must be a generally recognised and acceptable means of payment; as a commodity it must be durable; it must be portable; be available in different denominations; it must be of uniform quality; it must be difficult for individuals to produce themselves, such as in the case of paper money it must be difficult to forge.

11.3 What is money?

This may at first glance seem a rather strange question. It is quite obvious that in our society money is represented by the notes and coins in circulation. But what about other financial assets such as our accounts at the bank or building society, or even stocks and shares? Due to the difficulties in defining exactly what money is we must distinguish between **narrow** and **broad** definitions of money.

A narrow definition of money is one that includes only those assets that can be readily used to finance current spending, such as cash and cheque accounts (sight deposits).

A broad definition of money is one that contains a wider range of assets such as savings accounts. The assets in such accounts may differ in respect to how readily they can be converted into cash, this is known as the **liquidity** of an asset. Such accounts may require that a notice of withdrawal is given (time deposits).

When we attempt to measure the **money supply,** that is the total amount of money in the economy, we must decide what to include in our definition. This is a complex matter and has led to the calculation of a large number of monetary aggregates. Table 11.1 shows the size of the main measures of the money supply published by the Bank of England.

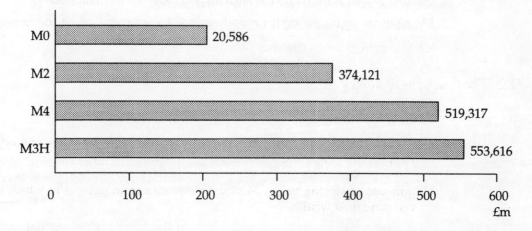

Table 11.1 Measures of the money supply in 1992

❑ **MO** is the narrowest definition of the money supply and includes notes and coins in circulation.

❑ **M2** is also classified as a narrow definition of the money supply and includes all sight deposits as well as MO.

❑ **M4** is a broad definition of the money supply and includes M2 plus deposits held in savings accounts.

❑ **M3H** is a very broad definition of money and includes M4 plus the holding of foreign currency deposits by UK residents. This measure of the money supply was devised by the central banks in the EU to aid comparisons between the performance of their different economies.

Part of government monetary policy may involve controlling the growth of the money supply. Given the measures identified above would it matter which the government selected as a basis of its policy action?

The answer is yes. The various measures of the money supply need not necessarily increase or decrease together. For example, if people shifted money from their sight deposits into time deposits, then M2 would fall whereas M4 would remain unchanged. Government tends to focus upon a number of measures of the money supply when deciding upon its policy action.

11.4 The banking system

At the top of the UK banking system is the Bank of England. The Bank of England performs a wide range of functions. These include:

- ❑ the issuing of notes and coins;
- ❑ acting as the banker to the government;
- ❑ acting as the banker to the commercial banks;
- ❑ managing the national debt and government borrowing;
- ❑ managing foreign currency reserves;
- ❑ supervising the activities of the banking system;
- ❑ advising the government on monetary policy;
- ❑ administering the governments monetary policy;
- ❑ acting as the lender of last resort.

As well as the Bank of England there are a number of other financial intermediaries, which are distinguished from one another on the basis of the deposits they take and to whom they lend.

- ❑ **Commercial banks** is the title given to the main high street banks, such as the National Westminster. They provide banking to the individual and specialise in providing cheque accounts. However, in recent years all the major commercial banks have diversified into many other areas of financial services, including personal loans and insurance.

- ❑ **Merchant banks** provide banking services to business. They specialise in providing large loans which might be drawn from a number of sources.

- ❑ **Savings banks** such as the Trustee Savings Bank (TSB), although set up initially to provide only saving facilities, have now expanded and become much like the main commercial banks, providing a wide range of financial services.

- ❑ **Building societies**, as the name implies, were set up to aid with the purchase of houses. Since the 1986 Building Societies Act their operations have expanded and, like the commercial and savings banks, they now offer a range of banking facilities such as cheque-book accounts.

❏ **Finance houses** specialise in providing loans for hire purchase agreements on large consumer items such as cars. Many finance houses are now run by the main commercial banks.

❏ **Discount houses** specialise in short term lending to the banking sector. They also act as the financial intermediary between the commercial banks and the Bank of England as well as providing a specialist market for issuing government debt in the form of treasury bills.

Activity

What is the difference between a capital market and a money market? Give examples of each.

The difference between capital and money markets is that:

❏ **capital markets** are concerned with long term finance;

❏ **money markets** are concerned with short term borrowing and lending.

Capital markets in the UK include:

❏ **the Stock Exchange**. The role of the stock exchange is to act as a market for companies that might wish to issue shares in order to raise finance. It also acts as a trading ground for shares already in circulation.

❏ **the guilt-edged market**. This is the market in which the government funds its spending by issuing government debt.

❏ **the Unlisted Securities Market**. Small to medium size firms that are unable to register on the stock exchange can issue shares and raise finance in this market.

The main money markets in the UK include:

❏ **the discount market**. In this market the discount houses buy and sell government securities.

❏ **the inter-bank market**. This market exists between the main commercial banks and enables them to lend short term funds to one another.

❏ **the eurocurrency market**. This market is for the buying and selling of foreign currency.

11.5 Credit creation and the money multiplier

So far in our discussion of money we have focused upon the problems of definition and the institutional arrangements concerning its trade. What is also important is understanding how, through the actions of the banking sector, changes can be made in the total amount of money in circulation. Changes in the money supply will have a significant impact upon the national economy.

The banking sector can influence the money supply through the process of **credit creation**.

Due to claims that investors have on banks, the banks will be forced to hold as cash a fraction of any new deposits in case of customer withdrawals. This is known as the **liquidity ratio** and represents the ratio of liquid to illiquid (lent) assets. Therefore when banks lend out funds, such funds will return to the banks as new deposits. A fraction of these new deposits will be put by as a cash reserve and the rest lent once more. This process will continue to repeat itself with a fraction of the same money being lent time after time. If bank deposits are included in our definition of the money supply then the money supply has clearly risen. In fact it has risen by a multiple of the initial increase in deposits. This is known as the **money multiplier** and can be found using the following formula $1/L$, where L is the liquidity ratio.

Activity

Assume that a banks cash reserve is 20%. What is the size of the money multiplier? Given an increase of £20m in new deposits complete the following table.

Round	New Deposits		
1	£20m	Hold	....
		Lend	....
2	....	Hold	....
		Lend	....
3	....	Hold	....
		Lend	....
4	....	Hold	....
		Lend	....
5	....	Hold	....
		Lend	....
Total Deposits	....		

The size of the money multiplier is 5. When you have completed the table correctly, the total level of deposits after five rounds should equal £67.27m. After each round the money lent will return as a new deposit. Given a money multiplier of 5 total deposits will eventually equal £100m.

11.6 The problem of inflation

Through the money multiplier a rise in bank lending will stimulate national expenditure. If the economy is running near full capacity the process of credit creation will simply feed through into higher prices. The average annual change in prices is known as **inflation** and is measured by a monthly calculation of the **Retail Price Index (RPI).**

The type of inflation resulting from a rise in the money supply can be classified as being **demand-pull**, more money means more purchasing power. Therefore prices are pulled upwards as the level of demand placed upon a given level of supply rises. Demand may also be pulled upwards through the actions of other variables such as injections of investment or government spending. In Figure 11.1a aggregate demand shifts right, both prices and the quantity produced increase. The nearer to full employment the more likely it is that inflation and not output will increase.

Alternatively inflation may result from **cost-push** pressures. Here we can distinguish between different types of cost pressure; wage-push, profit-push, import-push and tax-push. In this case firms which are facing rising costs will both cut back production but also pass some of the higher costs onto the consumer. In figure 11.1b we can see that higher costs cause the aggregate supply curve to shift left. Prices rise from P_e to P_{e2} and the quantity produced falls.

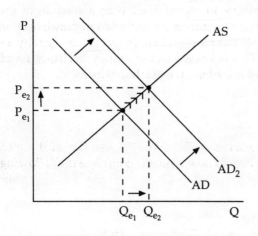 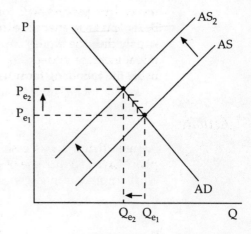

Figure 11.1a Demand pull inflation   *Figure 11.1b Cost push inflation*

Activity

Why is inflation considered to be undesirable?

The following arguments might be advanced to explain why inflation is undesirable:

❑ it creates **uncertainty** for businesses that need to plan for the future. If costs and profits are variable due to fluctuations in price then business will be reluctant to invest and take risks.

❑ rising prices undermine **international competitiveness**, this may have a detrimental effect upon the country's international trading position and its balance of payments.

❑ it affects the **distribution of income**, eroding the real value of earnings of those on fixed incomes, such as pensioners and those on state benefits.

11.7 For and against an independent central bank

The desire to achieve stable prices has pre-occupied government policy since the mid 1970's. The stability of prices and the effects this has on business expectations has come to be seen as the only long term way to create sustainable prosperity. The success of government via the use of traditional economic policy in achieving this goal has been mixed (see Chapter 12 for an assessment of economic policy). It has been suggested that what is in fact required is a substantial change in the institutional nature of the financial system, and in particular the Bank of England. The Bank of

England, it is argued, should become independent of government, much like the German Bundesbank, which has successfully controlled inflation for many years.

The arguments in favour of an independent central bank are:

☐ the bank would be free from the short run desires and manipulations of the politicians, in particular regarding interest rates, and hence free to pursue long term goals;

☐ independence would strengthen the credibility of monetary policy and help shape expectations;

☐ an independent bank would have a legal status separate from government. It would not be subordinate to it, and hence act as a check on government policy and actions.

Activity

What arguments might we advance against having an independent central bank?

The arguments against having an independent central bank are:

☐ the difficulty government would face in integrating monetary policy into a wider policy goal. For example, if the economy experienced high levels of unemployment, and it was deemed desirable for the economy to grow in order to create employment, then some inflationary pressure might be inevitable. If the independent bank responded by rising interest rates then this would be acting against the government's stimulus of the economy.

☐ to whom would bank officials be accountable to? Such individuals would have control over a very significant aspect of economic policy and yet not be democratically elected.

Whether or not we should have an independent central bank is unclear. Without one we have been relatively unsuccessful. Whether this would change with more independence is not at all certain.

Summary

In this chapter we have considered the role of money within the economy. We have looked at the functions of the various financial intermediaries and the implications of having an independent central bank. An understanding of these issues is vital if we are to appreciate the economic importance of money and its flow around the economy.

Further reading

Sloman J, *Economics*, Harvester Wheatsheaf, (1994), Chapters 18.

Progress questions

1. Four functions of money are: ....

....

2. Money is simply notes and coin in circulation.　　　True ☐ False ☐

3. The liquidity of an asset refers to the ease with which an asset can be converted to cash.

True ☐ False ☐

4. A narrow definition of the money supply is **MO/M4**. A broad definition of the money supply is **MO/M4**.

5. Five functions of The Bank of England might include: ....

....

6. Merchant banks provide services to business.　　　True ☐ False ☐

7. A discount house is where money can be picked up at a discount.

True ☐ False ☐

8. A CAPITAL/MONEY market is concerned with short term borrowing, whereas a CAPITAL/MONEY market is concerned with longer term finance.

9. The liquidity ratio is: ....

10. Inflation can be defined as: ....

....

Review questions

11. Why is the money supply so difficult to define? (Section 11.3)

12. List a range of financial intermediaries and explain their financial roles. (Section 11.4)

13. Explain how the process of credit creation operates. (Section 11.5)

14. Distinguish between demand-pull and cost push causes of inflation. (Section 11.6)

15. Outline the principal arguments both for and against having an independent central bank. (Section 11.7)

Multiple choice questions

16. Which of the following measures of the money supply has the greatest liquidity. Is it:

    (a) M2

    (b) M4

    (c) MO

    (d) M3H

17. A discount house is a specialist financial intermediary that deals in:

    (a) banking services to business.

    (b) offering mortgages.

    (c) finance for hire purchase agreements.

    (d) government debt.

18. Which of the following is **not** likely to lead to cost-push inflation.

    (a) Unions negotiate higher wages.

    (b) A fall in the rate of interest.

    (c) Government raises tax on company profits.

    (d) The price of raw materials rise.

Practice questions

19. Why is inflation considered to be an economic evil?

20. What impact would you expect the deregulation of the financial market to have upon government economic policy that attempts to control the money supply?

21. What factors might influence the level of credit creation within the economy?

Assignment

The link between money supply and inflation was a dominant theme in economic policy throughout the 1980's. However, the strength of the evidence concerning this link is far from clear. Using relevant data sources, such as Economic Trends, plot inflation over the 1980's, and then plot various measures of money supply. When plotting the money supply figures make sure you plot the percentage change from year to year. Does there appear to be a clear link between inflation and any measure of the money supply? Attempt to explain your findings?

12 Economic policy and the business environment

12.1 Introduction

The economic actions of government are crucial in shaping the environment in which businesses conduct their operations and devise there strategy. An understanding of such policy actions is necessary if business is to successfully predict the impact that any given change in policy might lead to.

On completing this chapter you should be able to:

❏ list the principle objectives of government economic policy;

❏ show how such objectives are related;

❏ outline the principal policy tools that government might adopt in pursuit of its main economic objectives;

❏ distinguish between interventionist and free market supply side policies.

12.2 The objectives of economic policy

There are four principal objectives of government economic policy. These are:

❏ **Economic growth**. A growing economy is often seen as an indicator of economic success. With a rising level of production the economy will experience a rising standard of living. As such governments will attempt not only to achieve growth but they will also aim to keep it stable and thereby avoid periods of recession.

❏ **Full employment**. Unemployed resources and in particular labour, is a sign of economic inefficiency. It also represents a large economic cost that society must carry in the form of welfare payments and the social effects of unemployment such as a rising level of poor health and its associated links with crime. Governments will attempt to achieve both a high and stable level of employment.

❏ **Stable prices**. Fluctuations in price create uncertainty. In an uncertain environment businesses will be unable to precisely predict their costs and subsequently derive their profits. The implications of this for variables such as investment, which may depend heavily upon profit assessments, is that businesses will be reluctant to invest. Therefore governments will attempt not only to keep price rises down but ensure that price fluctuations are minimised.

❏ **A balance of payments**. The balance of payments represents an account of a countries trading relations with the rest of the world. Governments will attempt to avoid a balance of payments deficit, that is a situation where imports exceed exports. A deficit represents a net flow of finance and hence wealth overseas. A balance of payments deficit cannot be maintained indefinitely as a country's reserves dwindle and borrowed money would simply mean the accumulation of debt. Therefore governments will aim to achieve a balance or a surplus of trade in the long run.

Although the four objectives listed represent the primary focus of government policy activity they do not represent the exclusive aims of government. Such a list could be extended to include objectives like the **distribution of income and wealth** and more recently, measures to protect the **environment**. Different governments will have different priorities and aims.

Activity

When a government enters office it will quickly discover that it cannot simultaneously achieve favourable outcomes in all its policy objectives. Such objectives will frequently conflict. As such government will be forced to prioritise, deciding which of its goals it will pursue. The dilemma facing government can be illustrated by looking at the trade cycle. In Figure 12.1 four phases of the trade cycle are identified; the recession, the upturn, the boom and the downturn.

Given the four objectives of government listed below identify in which phase of the cycle they are likely to be an issue of high or rising priority.

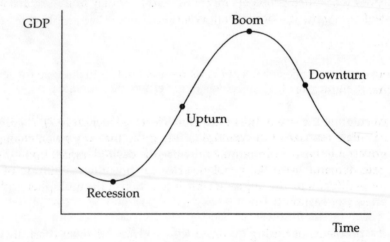

Figure 12.1 The trade cycle

In the recessionary phase of the cycle unemployment will be high and economic growth will be low. In the upturn the increase in prices will be a rising priority and the balance of payments will be shifting into deficit as consumer incomes rise. In the boom both inflation and the balance of payments will be key economic problems. In the downturn the converse will be true, slowing growth and rising unemployment will become more important objectives of government policy. We can see from this analysis that the objectives of government will largely be determined by the position of the economy in its trade cycle.

12.3 Policy instruments I: fiscal policy

In attempting to achieve its principal economic objectives government will need to use various **policy tools**. A wide variety of policy tools exist which can be classified as either focusing upon the **demand side** or the **supply side** of the economy.

The main demand side policies that government can use are **fiscal policy** and **monetary policy**. They are classified as demand side measures as they focus upon the control of consumer demand and income.

Fiscal policy involves the government manipulating its own budget, either through changes in taxation or government expenditure, to alter the level of aggregate demand within the economy (see section 10.4). If the government were to run a **budget deficit** this would in most cases represent a stimulus to the economy, conversely a **budget surplus** would act as a contraction on the level of demand. However, the **fiscal stance** of a budget, that is whether it is expansionary or contractionary, may also reflect the current state of the economy. For example, the governments budget will tend to move into deficit during a period of recession. Demands placed upon government expenditure will rise, as unemployment grows, and tax revenue falls as fewer are in employment. When the government runs a budget deficit the size of the deficit is referred to as the **public sector borrowing requirement (PSBR)**. If the government runs persistent deficits overtime, the accumulated debt is known as the **national debt**.

Activity

Before we focus upon the problems of using fiscal policy to manage demand, consider what such problems might be, and how they might reduce the effectiveness of government economic intervention.

There are three major problems in using fiscal policy to manage the level of aggregate demand, these are:

☐ calculating the size of the **multiplier effect** (see section 10.7). A failure to accurately calculate the size of the multiplier will mean that any given change in taxation or government expenditure may not have the desired impact upon the level of aggregate demand. Also the problem of calculating the magnitude of policy is made more difficult by the unpredictable interaction of the multiplier with the accelerator effect (see section 10.8).

☐ the problems of **timing**. In order for governments to successfully intervene in the running of the economy they must be able to predict the future path of economic activity. The reason for this is that all policy, and fiscal policy in particular, suffers from time lags. First there is a delay in policy as it takes time for government to recognise that a problem exists. It will then take time for government to act, and a further period of time for the policy imposed to have an effect. The economy in the mean time has continued along its trade cycle path. Government action, when it comes is based upon what the economy was doing in some previous time period and may not be sufficient to deal with the problem as it now stands. In the worse case scenario government policy may in fact have a detrimental effect, such as stimulating the economy once its has moved out of recession causing inflationary pressure to rise. This action will destabilize rather than stabilize the economy as intended.

☐ the problem of **crowding out**. If the government runs a budget deficit then it will require finance. It will finance its deficit by borrowing. Government, along with private business, will now be in competition for funds. The government borrows from the general public by issuing government stock such as bonds and bills which offer a given rate of interest. The larger the deficit the more bonds and bills issued and the higher the rate of interest that is required to encourage individuals to hold such government debt. This will push interest rates up throughout the economy and investment will be discouraged. As a consequence government spending is said to have crowded out private spending, and the net effect on the level of demand may well be zero as a consequence.

12.4 Policy instruments II: monetary policy

Monetary policy, as its name implies, is concerned with the control of finance within the economy. It focuses not only on the control of the **money supply**, but also encompasses the control of interest rates, credit and exchange rates.

Monetarist economists argue that a change in the supply of money will have a significant effect upon the performance of the economy. In order to conduct monetary policy the government will target a measure of the money supply (see section 11.3) which will act as an indicator of monetary growth and a guide for policy action. If monetary growth rises then this will stimulate aggregate demand. If monetary growth falls then this will contract aggregate demand. The government can attempt to control aggregate demand using three principle forms of monetary control. These are:

❑ the direct control of the money supply. In section 11.6 we discussed how, through the process of credit creation the banking system is able to stimulate the money supply. Monetary policy involves controlling the banks ability to do this and hence its liquidity ratio. This may be achieved in the following ways:

open market operations – involves the Bank of England buying and selling government securities on the open market. If the government wished to tighten monetary policy then it would sell more securities, which would be bought by individuals drawing money from their bank accounts. Banks will reduce their advances to customers as a consequence.

special deposits. The Bank of England can insist that the banks deposit a given percentage of any new deposit they receive with the Bank of England. Such deposits will only be released when the Bank of England is so instructed. As such banks must treat such special deposits as very illiquid and hence they must adjust their liquidity ratio and subsequent level of lending.

❑ the determination of interest rates. Interest rates influence the cost of borrowing. Control over the rate of interest will be an important means of controlling the total level of demand within the economy. The Bank of England can control the rate of interest through the operation of the discount market and the discount houses (see section 11.4). If the commercial banks run short of cash they will turn to the discount houses, who will in turn, if short of cash themselves, go to the Bank of England. The Bank of England will decide upon the rate of interest to charge the discount houses which will influence the rate of interest throughout the economy as a whole.

❑ the control of credit. The availability of credit will exert a considerable influence over individual spending decisions. As such an important aspect of monetary policy is the ability to ration the level of credit available. Banks can be requested to discriminate between borrowers or the government might impose strict credit controls such as a minimum level of deposit before credit can be offered.

Before we consider the problems government might encounter while using monetary policy, attempt to identify what the problems might be.

The problems experienced in conducting monetary policy will include:

❐ deciding which measure of the money supply to target. Should the measure be broad or narrow?

❐ banks will find ways around the restrictions imposed upon them.

❐ the deregulation of financial markets since 1979 has meant that the money supply can be influenced by many other financial institutions other than banks. As a result the financial system is far more difficult to control.

❐ the impact of interest rates upon the level of demand is uncertain. The businesses decision to invest and the consumers willingness to borrow will be determined by a wide range of factors such as confidence and expectations about the future, not just the cost of borrowing. For example, the progressive fall in interest rates since the UK left the ERM in September 1992, has not greatly stimulated the UK economy as anticipated. Business and consumer confidence has remained low and the economy as a consequence remained stagnant.

12.5 Policy instruments III: the supply side

Whereas fiscal and monetary policy focus upon the control of aggregate demand, supply side policy focuses upon the control of aggregate supply. Supply side policy can be classified as either free market orientated or interventionist. Free market supply side policy have been an important component of government policy action since 1979. The aim of such polices has been to remove market rigidities and encourage free market forces. Supply side policies since 1979 have included:

❐ attempts to reduce government expenditure. This has involved reducing many grants and subsidies, such as those to local authorities and the nationalised industries.

❐ privatisation and deregulation. Government policy has been to not only return many nationalised industries back to the private sector, which is believed to be more efficient, but to reduce controls and restrictions on many markets such as finance.

❐ the progressive reduction in personal taxation. High marginal rates of tax are argued to be a disincentive to work. As such the supply of labour to the market would be encouraged if such disincentives were removed.

❐ the removal of union rights. As well as high rates of income tax a further labour market restriction was suggested to be the activities of the union movement. Changes in the legal status of the trade union and its practices were seen as a way of not only controlling wages but allowing employers to more effectively manage their business organization.

❏ reductions in welfare and benefit provision. The provision of welfare benefits has been suggested by some to create a dependency culture, in which individuals lack the incentive to find employment. Therefore the wider the gap between state benefits and the wages from employment, the more encouragement the individual has to seek employment.

Activity

Not all supply side policies are focused upon the introduction of free market forces. Interventionist supply side policy can also be used to correct free market failures. What form might such policies take?

Interventionist supply side policy might include the following:

❏ **Regional policy** is a form of supply side policy that attempt to correct regional imbalances within the economy. Regional imbalance can arise due to the uneven development of industry, such as the location of heavy industry in the North of England. Such imbalance can be an important constraint upon general economic performance, and is frequently characterised by wide disparities in both the level of employment and income. During the 1980's the British economy experienced a growing divide between the north and south of the country as a consequence of the process of deindustrialization. The Government responded with regional policy measures that involved the direct provision of grants and subsidies to firms, encouraging them to locate in depressed economic regions, so generating both employment and rising levels of income.

❏ **Industrial policy** is a further form of interventionist supply side policy. It involves the attempt by government to improve the performance of industry. It might achieve this by offering investment grants, assistance with R&D, the provision of infrastructure, and in its most extreme form, industrial policy might even include the nationalisation of industry.

Summary

Government can attempt to control the economy either by focusing upon demand or supply side policy. It is likely that government in an attempt to achieve its economic goals will use a policy package that will contain a variety of policy tools. It is only by using such a package that it is likely to be successful in managing economic affairs.

Further reading

Sloman J, *Economics*, Harvester Wheatsheaf, (1994) Chapters 17, 19 and 22 selectively.

Hare P and Simpson L, *British Economic Policy*, Harvester Wheatsheaf, (1993), Chapters 2 and 3.

Progress questions

1. The four principal objectives of government are: ....
....

2. When the economy is growing the balance of payments are moving into deficit.

   True ☐ False ☐

3. When we have low inflation unemployment will tend to be high.

   True ☐ False ☐

4. A demand side policy is so called because: ....

   ....

5. The government's fiscal stance is: ....

   ....

6. Crowding out refers to the government using up to many resources.

   True ☐ False ☐

7. If the government wished to tighten monetary policy it would SELL/BUY more government securities.

8. If the government wished to relax monetary policy it would SELL/BUY more government securities.

9. Five forms of free market supply side policy are: ....

   ....

10. Nationalisation is a supply side policy.

   True ☐ False ☐

Review questions

11. How are the economic objectives of government shaped by the business cycle? (Section 12.2)

12. Explain how fiscal policy can be used to control the level of demand within the economy. (Section 12.3)

13. Why is the impact of monetary policy on the level of demand, in particular following changes in the rate of interest, less easy to predict? (Section 12.4)

14. Distinguish between demand side and supply side policy. Give examples. (Section 12.5)

15. Outline a case for and against the use of free market supply side policy. (Section 12.5)

Multiple choice questions

16. The fiscal stance of the government refers to:
    (a) the level of taxation the government sets.
    (b) how much it spends.
    (c) the level of borrowing it must raise.
    (d) the expansionary or contractionary state of its budget.

17. Which of the following is **not** a form of monetary policy.
    (a) Open market operations.
    (b) Special deposits.
    (c) The progressive reduction in personal taxation.
    (d) The control of credit

18. Which of the following is **not** an example of supply side policy?
    (a) Privatisation.
    (b) The offering of regional economic grants.
    (c) A cut in welfare benefits.
    (d) A rise in the rate of interest.

Practice questions

19. "The problems with fiscal policy mean that its impact upon the economy will be highly uncertain." Explain and evaluate this statement.

20. Why would an effective economic policy incorporate both demand and supply side policies?

21. How might economic events in foreign countries, such as a rise in Japanese interest rates, influence domestic economic policy?

Assignment

In this assignment you are to investigate more fully the various supply side measures undertaken since 1979, and attempt to evaluate their impact upon the economy. In assessing the impact of such policy you will need to focus upon the markets for goods and services, as well as labour and finance. In your evaluation you should clearly highlight the advantages and disadvantages that the various supply side policy have created. Various chapters in this book will act as a good guide to some of the problems you will need to consider.

13 *The international dimension*

13.1 *Introduction*

In an open economy where foreign trade is an important part of business activity, the economic decision-making process, both within business and government, must consider international economic relations. Over recent years as international trade has expanded, economies world-wide have become more interdependent. Economic changes in one part of the world now have a dramatic effect on business activity elsewhere.

On completing this chapter you should be able to:

❏ define what is meant by the terms of trade;

❏ analyse a balance of payments account;

❏ describe what is meant by an exchange rate and identify different forms of exchange rate regime;

❏ distinguish between protectionism and free trade;

❏ define what is meant by international policy co-operation and show how such co-operation might be practised;

❏ state the principles of the General Agreement on Tariffs and Trade (GATT) and assess its performance in freeing world trade.

13.2 *Imports, exports and the terms of trade*

Countries are linked via the import and export of goods, services, commodities and capital. Whether such trade is benefiting a country can be assessed by reference to a country's **terms of trade**. This is the quantity of foreign goods a country can get in exchange for a given quantity of its own goods. Thus if a country gets more imports for a given quantity of its own exports, then the terms of trade are moving in its favour. The terms of trade are calculated by dividing the price of exports by the price of imports.

Activity

Using the following formula:

$$\frac{\text{Index of average price of exports}}{\text{Index of average price of imports}} \times 100$$

calculate from the data below the terms of trade for the UK economy, and assess whether trade is moving in Britain's favour or not.

Year	Export unit value Index	Import unit value Index	Terms of Trade
1980	69.9	67.8	....
1981	76.2	73.7	....
1982	81.4	79.9	....
1983	88.0	87.4	....
1984	95.0	95.3	....
1985	100.0	100.0	....
1986	90.1	95.4	....
1987	93.5	98.0	....
1988	93.4	96.9	....
1989	100.8	104.1	....
1990	106.2	108.0	....
1991	106.4	108.4	....

Since 1985 the terms of trade have moved against the UK, reaching a low of 94.4 in 1986. Although the terms of trade have improved since, we are still receiving fewer goods in exchange for our exports.

13.3 The balance of payments

The **balance of payments** is an account which records all the monetary transactions between the UK and the rest of the world over a given period of time, usually a year. It is split into a **current account** and a **capital account**. The current account comprises a further two sections; trade in goods or **visible items** and trade in services or **invisible items**. The difference between the level of visible exports and visible imports is known as the **balance of trade** and represents the largest section of the balance of payments account. The invisible balance looks at trade in travel, financial services, and the payments of profits and dividends.

The capital account balances aspects of investment and borrowing between countries. It includes monies used in short-term capital movement for speculation, and long-term capital investments. It also includes debits and credits in the UK's reserves of gold and foreign currency, which change in response to government intervention in the foreign exchange market.

The current account and the capital account should balance when they are added together. However, omissions and errors which may occur can be accounted for by using a **balancing item**. Depending upon whether there is a balance of payments **surplus** (exports are greater than imports) or a balance of payments **deficit** (imports are greater than exports) this will have implications for government policy, the exchange rate and ultimately the performance of business overseas.

Activity

Table 13.1 below is a summary of the UK's balance of payments account since 1980. What does the data tell us about the UK's economic performance overseas? (Note: a desirable balance of payments position is as mentioned in section 12.2 when the accounts are roughly in balance or slight surplus. A balance of payments deficit is to be avoided).

Year	Exports (f.o.b.)	Imports (f.o.b.)	Visible balance	Invisible balance	Current balance	Net transactions in UK assets & liabilities	Other recorded transactions	Balancing item
1980	47,149	45,792	1,357	1,487	2,844	3,940	180	916
1981	50,668	47,416	3,252	3,496	6,748	7,436	158	530
1982	55,331	53,421	1,910	2,741	4,651	2,519		−2,132
1983	60,700	62,237	−1,573	5,302	3,765	4,562		797
1984	70,265	75,601	−5,336	7,134	1,798	8,414		6,616
1985	77,991	81,336	−3,345	6,136	2,791	3,733		842
1986	72,627	82,186	−9,559	9,625	66	3,134		3,068
1987	79,153	90,735	−11,582	7,099	−4,483	4,334		149
1988	80,346	101,826	−21,480	5,302	−16,189	9,396		6,782
1989	92,154	116,837	−24,683	2,956	−21,727	19,255		2,472
1990	101,718	120,527	−18,809	1,778	−17,031	11,091		5,940
1991	103,413	113,703	−10,290	3,905	−6,385	6,644		−259
1992	106,775	120,546	−13,771	1,857	−11,914	2,436		9,478

Source: Economic Trends

Table 13.1 The balance of payments since 1980

The UK's visible balance has been in deficit since 1983. This was compensated until 1987 by a surplus in invisible trade. However, in 1987 the current account as a whole slipped into deficit, which has since grown rapidly. In 1989 the deficit stood at £21,727m, the worst in UK history.

13.4 The balance of payments and the exchange rate

In order to understand why deficits and surplus occur within the balance of payments we need to consider the market for foreign exchange and the determination of the **exchange rate**.

The exchange rate is the rate at which one currency can be traded for another. The rate of exchange is determined on the foreign exchange market by the demand and supply of a particular currency. If foreigners want to buy British goods, they will demand £ sterling to do so. They buy £ sterling by exchanging it for their own currency. The rate of exchange tells them how many pounds they will get for their money. If the exchange rate is £1 = $1.89, an American would need to give $1.89 for every £1 purchased. Alternatively, if we wished to buy imports or invest overseas then we would need to supply £ sterling to the market to convert it into foreign currency. With the exchange rate above we would get $1.89 for every pound we supplied. As in any market situation if there is an excess supply of sterling the exchange rate falls; if there is excess demand, the exchange rate rises.

The advantages of having a high rate of exchange are that:

❏ import prices will be low as we get more foreign goods for every pound;

❏ higher priced UK exports will force UK business to be more cost competitive and hence more efficient in order to trade overseas.

The disadvantages of having a high rate of exchange are that:

❏ UK exports are less competitive on international markets therefore the balance of payments is likely to move into deficit;

❏ as UK business becomes less competitive overseas many may be forced out of business, this could lead to rising unemployment in the long term.

The advantages of having a low rate of exchange are that:

❏ increased competitiveness abroad could help stimulate business investment and help expand the domestic economy;

❏ domestically produced products are relatively cheaper than imports, this could stimulate domestic demand;

❏ the balance of payments may move into surplus.

The disadvantages of having a low rate of exchange are that:

❏ higher import prices will cause costs to rise hence stimulating a rise in the level of inflation;

❏ UK businesses can maintain their export sales without improving productivity and hence becoming more efficient.

Activity

Table 13.2 shows the value of sterling against a range of other currencies since 1980. The effective exchange rate in the final column is a weighted average exchange rate value derived from a basket of currencies. The weights of the currencies included in the basket are determined by the level of trade conducted with each country.

What has been happening to the value of sterling since 1980?

| | Sterling exchange rate against major currencies | | | | | | | | UK official Sterling | |
	Japanese yen	US dollar	Swiss franc	European currency (ECU)	French franc	Italian lira	Deutsche-mark	Spanish peseta	reserves at end of period (£ m)	exchange rate index (average 1985=100)
1985	307.08	1.2976	3.155	1.6998	11.5495	2,463	3.784	219.56	15,543	100.0
1986	246.80	1.4672	2.635	1.4948	10.1569	2,186	3.183	205.31	21,923	91.5
1987	236.50	1.6392	2.439	1.4200	9.8369	2,123	2.941	201.87	44,326	90.1
1988	227.98	1.7796	2.603	1.5060	10.5969	2,315	3.124	207.16	51,685	95.5
1989	225.66	1.6383	2.678	1.4886	10.4476	2,247	3.079	193.88	38,645	92.6
1990	257.38	1.7864	2.469	1.4000	9.6891	2,133	2.876	181.29	38,464	91.3
1991	237.56	1.7685	2.529	1.4584	9.9473	2,187	2.925	183.22	44,126	91.7
1992	223.72	1.7665	2.476	1.3620	9.3248	2,163	2.751	179.91	41,654	88.4
1993	166.73	1.5015	2.218	1.2845	8.5073	2,360	2.483	191.33	42,926	80.2

Source: Economic Trends

Table 13.2 The value of sterling since 1985

The value of sterling in general against all the listed currencies, has fallen. The exchange rate index suggests the pound has fallen on average by 20% since 1985. Reread the section above to assess the implications for the UK economy.

13.5 The determination of exchange rates

In a system of **floating** exchange rates, exchange rate values are determined by market forces. This not only ensures that the demand for and supply of sterling are equal, but also that the debits on the balance of payments are equal to the credits. If there was a balance of payments deficit then imports (debits) would exceed exports (credits). The supply of sterling to the foreign exchange market to buy imports would be greater then the demand for sterling to buy UK exports. As a consequence the value of the sterling exchange rate would fall, exports would become more competitive and imports more expensive. At some point in the future the balance of payments would move out of its deficit situation and back to balance, where the demand for sterling was equal to the supply of sterling. In a system of floating exchange rates a fall in the value of a currency is known as a **depreciation** and rise in the value of the exchange rate as an **appreciation**.

In most cases however foreign exchange rates are not left to the determination of market forces. Governments frequently intervene to solve balance of payments disequilibria, and to regulate exchange rate fluctuations. They do this as an attempt to improve the decision making environment for business by reducing the uncertainty that accompanies trading overseas. There are a variety of possible ways to intervene and attempt to fix the rate of exchange.

Short term intervention can include:

❐ the use of reserves of gold and foreign currency to buy and sell pounds on the open market;

❐ raise or lower interest rates to persuade or dissuade investors from depositing money in the economy.

Long term intervention can include:

❐ direct controls on the flow of goods, services and capital both into and out of the country, such as through the use of tariffs, quotas and exchange control regulations;

❐ deflationary/reflationary measures which regulate the level of domestic spending;

❐ devaluation/revaluation may be possible in a system of fixed exchange rates. By devaluing or revaluing a currency the price of foreign currency is adjusted and the competitive position of the country can subsequently be made to improve or deteriorate.

For an example of a managed exchange rate see section 14.4 which considers the operation of the European Exchange Rate Mechanism (ERM).

Activity

What will happen to the value of the exchange rate given the following conditions (assume that exchange rates are floating):

i) A UK inflation rate higher than abroad;

ii) A fall in the level of income in the UK;

iii) UK interest rate rise;

iv) American interest rates rise;

v) Business expectations are that the UK economy is entering a recessionary period.

(i) If the UK inflation rate is higher than overseas, British goods are relatively less competitive. The demand for pounds will fall, causing the exchange rate to drop. (ii) If income falls in the UK, the demand for imports and therefore the supply of sterling to the foreign exchange market will fall. This will cause the exchange rate to rise. (iii) If

115

UK interest rates rise, then holding sterling balances becomes more profitable. The demand for sterling will increase, forcing the exchange rate to rise. (iv) A rise in American interest rates will cause the demand for sterling to fall as people will wish to hold dollar balances. (v) If it is anticipated that the British economy is due to enter a recession, the demand for sterling will fall, pushing the exchange rate down.

13.6 Protectionism and free trade

As well as the value of the exchange rate access into foreign markets will also have an important impact upon the businesses performance overseas. Various arguments have been put forward both to support and criticise the use of protectionist trade measures.

Those in favour of **protectionism** argue that:

- it is an effective way to deal with imported goods that are being **dumped** on the domestic market. Dumped goods are those that are being sold at below cost price, hence threatening the performance of domestic producers;

- it helps to protect **infant industries**. Infant industries are new and likely to have higher costs than well established overseas producers. Hence protectionism is necessary if they are to secure a position in the domestic market and be competitive with foreign firms in the long run;

- certain **strategic industries** must be protected in the national interest. The protectionist policies surrounding agriculture in Europe were established on the grounds that it was vital to be self-sufficient in food production;

- many **old or senile industries** need protection in order to prevent their collapse in the face of foreign competition. Such industries may be significant employers of labour and their closure would lead to many undesirable economic side effects. Therefore protectionism can be used as a means of safeguarding such industries while alternative forms of employment and production are developed.

The following arguments have been advanced against the use of protectionist measures:

- protectionism will lead to **retaliation**. The consequence of this is that the volume of world trade will fall and so will the growth rates of countries;

- the use of protectionist measures produces **ill-will** between countries which can spill over into other areas where countries might co-operate, such as in the political sphere;

- protectionism removes foreign competition which might act as a stimulus to domestic firms to become more efficient.

Activity

If a country was to practice protectionism, what forms might such protectionism take?

There are a wide variety of measures open to government if it wished to restrict trade.

These include the use of:

☐ **tariffs**. A tariff is a tax placed upon imported goods or services. Tariffs not only raise the price of imports relative to domestic products but they also raise revenue for government.

☐ **quotas**. A quota is a restriction placed upon how much of a good can be imported.

☐ **exchange controls**. Exchange controls are used to limit the availability of foreign currency for those who wish to import.

☐ **subsidies**. Subsidies can be given either to exporters, who can lower their export price or domestic producers who can more effectively compete with cheaper imports.

☐ **administrative barriers**. Such barriers can include the setting of health and safety standards or insisting on specific product specifications.

☐ **embargoes**. At the most extreme level of protectionism imported goods can be banned from entering the market.

13.7 International policy co-operation

During the interwar years 1918-1939, world trade collapsed as it sank into protectionism. This contributed in large part to what we now call **The Great Depression**. As countries restricted trade economic growth fell, the level of world demand dropped and unemployment increased. This vicious spiral proved difficult to break.

Following the turmoil of World War II, the desire to avoid protectionism and quickly establish a stable world economic system saw the creation of two new institutions to help manage world economic affairs. They were the **International Monetary Fund (IMF)** and the **World Bank**.

The IMF was initially conceived to help manage the new exchange rate devised at Bretton Woods in 1944. It was to hold a fund of reserves, contributed by members, and was to act as a lender in times of crisis. It's role today is not fundamentally different, although it's importance in international affairs has declined significantly over the 1970's and 1980's. Today the IMF's role centres around the management of third world debt, acting either as a direct provider of funds or as a intermediary between debtor nations and creditors.

The World Bank was established at the same time as the IMF. Although it was not formally operating until 1947. It's initial role was to aid in the post war reconstruction of Europe by supplying loans and credit for development projects. As with the IMF the World Bank is financed via funds from member countries. Whereas the IMF's role has changed over time, the World Bank remains the provider of funds for development projects, although as with the IMF, its operations are increasingly based in less developed countries.

Political and financial constraints have restricted the effectiveness of the IMF and the World Bank and with the liberalisation of capital and financial markets, it is becoming increasingly easy for countries to arrange commercial credit for themselves.

Co-operation between nations through international agencies such as the IMF and World Bank are not the only basis for co-operative action. Nations might attempt to:

☐ exchange information on economic performance;

☐ co-ordinate consistent economic policies;

☐ embark upon joint action to achieve mutually agreed goals, such as exchange rate values.

The greater the degree of co-operation between nations the greater the realisation that their economies are interdependent and that the actions of one nation will have implications for others.

One organisation which has proved to be highly effective in respect to co-ordinating policy action and improving international trade has been the General Agreement on Tariffs & Trade (GATT). The GATT was established in 1948 with the aim to encourage free trade by removing tariffs and abolishing quota restrictions. Initially GATT had 23 member countries, today there are over 100 countries that account for 90% of the worlds trade. Members of GATT meet periodically for rounds of talks which take place over a period of years. There have been eight such rounds, the most successful being the Kennedy round (1964-7) and the Tokyo round (1973-79). Both saw significant reductions in the level of tariff barriers.

The most recent round of talks known as the Uruguay round (1986-94) have been proved to be the most difficult to resolve. The complexity of the issues, and the interests of different groups of countries, made the failure of GATT seem a real possibility. The four main issues of the Uruguay round were:

❐ textiles;

❐ agriculture;

❐ trade in services;

❐ intellectual property.

Agriculture proved to be the biggest problem to resolve. The EU, with its highly subsidised agricultural sector refused to remove all support for its agricultural products as first requested by the USA, whose farmers were unable to compete with fellow state aided European farmers. The EU's opposition was due to the fact that many farmers within it had become dependent upon state aid and its removal would drive them out of business. A compromise solution was eventually reached after much argument and the GATT round was concluded and hailed a success.

The future of GATT following the problems of the Uruguay round is uncertain. In recent times many countries have shifted back towards protectionist policies. This has not been helped by the establishment of trading blocs such as the EU (see chapter 14), and the creation of the **North American Free Trade Agreement (NAFTA)** between the USA, Canada and Mexico. Such blocs are frequently inward looking, and adopt many forms of hidden protectionism, outside the sphere of GATT discussions, such as product specifications. Such measures can be just as effective in restricting the level of imports and the extent of overseas competition that a country or group of countries might face.

Activity

Why might countries find it difficult to co-ordinate and co-operate with other nations?

There are a variety of reasons that you might have identified. These could include; deciding and clarifying what problems they face; deciding how best such problems could be dealt with; attempting to reconcile the pressures of domestic political issues and international agreements.

Summary

In this chapter we have considered a number of issues that face the business when it considers trading overseas. The determination of exchange rates and the use of protectionist trade policies are beyond the control of the individual business and are dictated by the policy of government, whether in the UK or overseas.

Further reading

Livesey F, *Economics*, Longman, (1991) Chap 25.

Hare P and Simpson L, *British Economic Policy*, Harvester Wheatsheaf, (1993), Chap 6.

Progress questions

1. The terms of trade refers to: ....

    ....

2. The current account of the balance of payments is comprised of visible and invisible trade.

    True ☐ False ☐

3. The rate of exchange is the rate at which one currency is traded for another.

    True ☐ False ☐

4. Two advantages of a high valued pound are: ....

    ....

5. High import prices will result from a RISE/FALL in the value of the pound.

6. A fall in the value of the pound in a floating exchange rate system is known as a DEPRECIATION/DEVALUATION.

7. Three forms of long term intervention to correct the balance of payments will include: ....

    ....

8. The existence of an infant industry is an argument in favour of protectionism.

    True ☐ False ☐

9. Three arguments against protectionism include: ....

    ....

10. Three international organizations that have improved international policy co-ordination are: ....

Review questions

11. How are the exchange rate and the balance of payments linked? (Section 13.4)

12. Explain how a floating exchange rate is determined. (Section 13.5)

13. Government intervention to solve balance of payments problems can involve using either short or long term policy. Distinguish between them and offer examples. (Section 13.5)

14. Outline a case both for and against free trade. (Section 13.6)

15. Why do countries find it difficult to co-ordinate international economic policy? (Section 13.7)

Multiple choice questions

16. A countries terms of trade refers to:

    (a) the quantity of foreign goods gained form a given quantity of its own goods.

    (b) the level of protection it uses against imported goods.

    (c) the formal agreements a country has with its trading partners.

    (d) the position of the balance of payments.

17. A high exchange rate will mean that:

    (a) imports are cheap.

    (b) the balance of payments is likely to move towards surplus.

    (c) businesses will be highly price competitive on overseas markets.

    (d) the economy will be experiencing imported inflation.

18. Which of the following is **not** an advantage of protectionism.

    (a) Infant industries are protected.

    (b) Protected industries will be more efficient.

    (c) The national interest can be safeguarded.

    (d) Senile industries have time to restructure their business activities.

Practice questions

19. Assess the advantages and disadvantages of having either a fixed or a floating exchange rate.

20. "Free trade only benefits economically dominant countries." Explain and assess.

21. What current international economic issues does the world economy face? How might a co-ordinated world economic policy deal with such problems?

Assignment

In this chapter we have tended to focus upon the international economic relations between the developed economies of the world. In this assignment you are to present a profile of two developing countries, one from Africa, and one from Latin America. In your analysis you should consider what particular economic problems they face and why the international economy might be so important to their economic development? Statistical sources you might use include The World Bank Annual Report, Economist Country Reports and various OECD statistical sources.

14 European community and the business environment

14.1 Introduction

As shown in Chapter 13, intervention is an important part of modern international trade, and the movement towards the creation of free trade areas, such as the European Union (EU), will have important implications for business and its foreign trading environment. In this chapter we will explore some of the implications of European union for British business.

On completing this chapter you should be able to:

☐ describe how the EU is organized;

☐ outline the issues surrounding the EU's budget;

☐ analyse how EU economic policies will influence the performance of business;

☐ describe what is meant by the term monetary union and how it is to be completed;

☐ outline the main points of the Maastricht treaty;

☐ describe the operation, performance and problems with the European exchange rate mechanism (ERM).

14.2 The European Union

The European Community (EC) was formed in 1958 following the signing of the Treaty of Rome. It originally consisted of six member countries, Belgium, France, Italy, Luxembourg, the Netherlands and West Germany. Today there are some 12 members, including, Denmark, Ireland, the United Kingdom, Greece, Spain and Portugal. The UK joined in 1973. The aim of the EC is to ultimately create an economic union, in which all policies between member states would be harmonized, this might include the existence of a single currency and a single European bank to run monetary affairs. This goal was to be achieved in stages. The initial stage was to establish a 'common market', that is a market free from trade restrictions between member countries. Such an agreement would cover not just goods and services but capital and labour. With the signing of the Single European Act (SEA) in 1985 and its implementation in December 1992, this initial stage is virtually complete.

The organisation of the EU is based around four principal institutions. These are:

☐ **The European Commission**. The European Commission is the EU's civil service. It has no political power and functions merely as a policy formulator and administrator.

☐ **The Council of Ministers**. There are 12 ministers, each one representing a member country. The council has significant power and is the forum where EU policy is ratified. Important pieces of legislation will be ratified by heads of state.

❏ **European Parliament**. The European parliament has 518 members. Although its powers have been enhanced by the Maastricht Treaty (see section 14.4) it is only able to influence certain areas of legislation.

❏ **The European Court of Justice**. The court has 13 judges and significant powers in being able to overrule legal decisions made in member countries.

The EU's budget is agreed annually and raised from four sources (the figures in brackets represent the percentage contribution to finance in 1991):

❏ duties imposed upon imported non-EU produced goods (22.6%);

❏ levies imposed upon imported agricultural foodstuffs (4.8%);

❏ the imposing of VAT (54%);

❏ contributions by member states, up to 1.2% of GNP (13.2%).

Even given these sources the EU's budget is in fact very small. In 1992 it represented only 1.2% of the total GNP of all members.

Activity

In respect to areas of expenditure, table 14.1 below highlights the main demands placed upon the EU's budget. What do the figures on EU expenditure suggest?

Sector	1980		1983		1985		1988		1990	
	Mio ECU	%	Mio ECU	%	Mio ECU	%	Mio ECU	%	Mio ECU	%
EAGGF Guarantee*	11485.5	71.0	15811.0	63.7	19955.0	70.2	27500.0	62.8	26431.0	56.3
Agricultural structures	328.7	2.0	653.4	2.6	687.7	2.4	1222.0	2.8	2073.5	4.4
Fisheries	64.1	0.4	84.4	0.3	111.7	0.4	271.0	0.6	358.6	0.8
Regional policy	722.7	4.5	2383.0	9.5	1697.8	6.0	3201.4	7.3	5209.7	11.1
Social policy	768.8	4.8	1495.1	6.0	1626.2	5.7	2845.3	6.5	3667.0	7.8
Research, energy	379.5	2.3	1386.5	5.5	706.8	2.5	1153.6	2.6	1733.4	3.7
Development co-operation	641.6	4.0	992.2	4.0	1043.7	3.7	870.5	2.0	1489.6	3.2
Administration	938.8	5.8	1161.6	4.6	1332.6	4.7	1967.2	4.5	2381.3	5.1
Miscellaneous	852.8	5.3	1093.8	4.4	1271.8	4.5	4779.4	10.9	3584.3	7.6
Total budget	16182.5	100.0	25061.1	100.0	28433.2	100.0	43820.4	100.0	46928.4	100.0

*European Agricultural Guarantee and Guidance Fund.

Source: Commission of the EC, 'The Community Budget: The Facts in Figures', various issues
Table 14.1 The structure of the EU budget, 1980–1990

Agriculture is by a considerable margin the largest consumer of expenditure and has been the subject of much internal debate and reform. Even though agriculture's share of the budget has fallen it is still the most significant consumer of EU funds.

14.3 The EU and economic policy

The three areas where the EU has a significant impact upon business activity are **competition policy**, **regional aid** and **monetary union**.

Competition Policy. The influence of European competition policy on business was discussed in section 3.8. It's principal aim is to prevent competitive practices that might distort competition between member states and so restrict the successful economic integration of Europe.

Regional Policy. Within the EU there exist wide regional disparities both between and within countries. Such regional disparities might be reflected in higher rates of unemployment or low levels of per capita income. If left to the free play of market forces it is unlikely that such disparities will be removed. In fact the gap between rich and poor is likely to widen. The imperfect nature of markets such as the immobility of both capital and labour means that wealthy regions will tend to prosper and depressed regions will tend to stagnate. Hence an internal free market that benefits all member states requires that assistance is given to those regions that need help.

European regional initiatives have been in operation since 1975, however it is only with the entry of Spain and Portugal in 1986 that regional issues have become more prominent. In 1989 policy initiatives in a number of different areas, such as the European Regional Development Fund and the European Social Fund, were to be subject to greater co-ordination and form what is now called **structural policy**. As well as these changes, funds to structural policy are expected to increase substantially, reaching 34% of the communities budget in 1997.

Monetary Union. The European Monetary System (EMS) was set up in March 1979, it's aim was to aid not only monetary union but to help create monetary stability through managing the level of exchange rates (see section 14.6). The EMS was however only a temporary step towards achieving monetary union. In 1989 The Delors Report set out three stages to achieve such a union.

Stage 1. The establishment of the SEA; tighter competition policy; improved monetary policy co-ordination; the joining of all member countries to the ERM; the deregulation of financial markets.

Stage 2. The strengthening of EU institutions; formation of a European system of central banks.

Stage 3. EU exchange rates to be fixed; eventual introduction of a single currency and a single central bank.

The potential gains from such a union were considered to be extensive. The Ceccini Report (1988) suggested that the following benefits would accrue from stage 1 and the formation of the single market:

❏ gains in wealth of between 4–6%;

❏ price reductions by on average 6%

❏ a 1% improvement in Europe's external trade;

❏ 1.8m new jobs.

The Maastricht Treaty, debated over in December 1991 and signed in February 1992, represented a further significant step towards European union. It sought to establish and clarify how monetary union was to be achieved and outline the key criteria that were necessary for successful economic convergence.

The following convergence criteria were identified:

❏ a stable exchange rate that had not been devalued for at least two years;

❏ a high degree of price stability, in which inflation does not exceed by more than 1.5% the three best-performing member states;

❏ a sustainable government financial position, in which the governments budget deficit is no greater than 3% of GDP.

❏ a rate of interest, over the long term, that does not exceed by more than 2% the three best-performing member states on price stability.

Activity

As well as the monetary union aspects of the Maastricht Treaty, it also contained a range of other issues, set out below:

❏ the powers of the European parliament were to be extended to policy areas such as transport, social policy, R&D and the environment;

❏ social policy in the form of the social chapter extended a European wide initiative to establish common health and safety conditions, wages and other worker rights;

❏ the establishment of a common foreign and security policy;

❏ the creation of a common immigration policy.

Assess the implications such measures might have for business and its performance.

The impact of the Maastricht treaty upon UK business is unclear. The 'opt-out' clauses negotiated by the UK, in both the spheres of monetary union and the social chapter, mean that agreements in these areas will not directly affect UK business or the UK economy. However, other EU directives, such as those for example governing pollution emissions, will create a European wide standard. This could well entail higher costs as producers are forced to conform with stricter EU guidelines. Given the high level of trade that the UK now has with the EU, UK business would be forced to improve efficiency to remain competitive.

14.4 The ERM and the future of monetary union

A crucial component of monetary union is the European exchange rate mechanism. The ERM represents a form of **semi-fixed exchange rate**. The linking of exchange rate values will:

❏ encourage trade between member countries as the risks of foreign trade are minimised;

❏ see member countries act in support of each others currency in the face of speculation.

The ERM was formed as part of the EMS in 1979. Britain did not join at this time preferring to opt for more policy independence. The ERM operated by first denominating all member's currencies in **ECUs (European currency units)**. The value of the ECU was determined by a basket of currencies, each with a different weight according to its importance as a trading currency. Members then agreed on a value of the ECU, a central rate, against which their currencies were allowed to fluctuate within a band of + or – 2.25% (when the UK and Spain entered the ERM in 1990 there were given a band of + or – 6%). Hence the French franc for example would not be allowed to be 2.25% stronger than the weakest currency nor 2.25% weaker than the strongest currency. If the currency reached either the upper or lower band then the central banks would intervene to help reduce speculative pressure. This intervention was signalled by the use of a **parity grid** which identified the bands each currency had relative to other member's currencies. A parity grid is shown in table 14.2.

		B.Fc/L.Fc 100	D.Kr. 100	Fr.Fc. 100	DM 100	I£ 1	Lit1,000	Fl 100	Pts 100	£1
Belgium/ Luxembourg	S	–	553.000	628.970	2109.50	56.5115	28.1930	1872.15	33.6930	64.6050
	C	–	540.723	614.977	2062.55	55.2545	27.5661	1830.54	31.7316	60.8451
B.Fc./L.Fc.	B	–	528.70	601.295	2016.55	54.0250	26.9530	1789.85	29.8850	57.3035
Denmark	S	18.9143	–	116.320	390.160	10.4511	5.21400	346.240	6.23100	11.9479
	C	18.4938	–	113.732	381.443	10.2186	5.09803	338.537	5.86837	11.2526
D.Kr.	B	18.0831	–	111.200	373.000	9.9913	4.98500	331.020	5.52600	10.5976
France	S	16.6310	89.9250	–	343.050	9.18900	4.58450	304.440	5.47850	10.50550
	C	16.2608	87.9257	–	335.920	8.98480	4.48247	297.661	5.15981	9.89389
Fr.Fc.	B	15.8990	85.9700	–		8.78500	4.38300	291.040	4.85950	9.31800
Germany	S	4.95900	26.8100	30.4950	–	2.74000	1.36700	90.7700	1.63300	3.13200
	C	4.84837	26.2162	29.8164	–	2.67894	1.33651	88.7526	1.53847	2.95000
DM	B	4.74000	25.6300	29.1500	–	2.61900	1.30650	86.7800	1.44900	2.77800
Ireland	S	1.85100	10.00870	11.3830	38.1825	–	0.510246	33.8868	0.609772	1.16920
	C	1.80981	9.78604	11.1299	37.3281	–	0.498895	33.1293	0.574281	1.10118
I£	B	1.76950	9.56830	10.8825	36.4964	–	0.487799	32.3939	0.540858	1.03710
Italy	S	3710.20	20062.0	22817.0	76540.0	2050.03	–	67912.0	1222.30	2343.62
	C	3627.64	19615.0	22309.1	74821.7	2004.43	–	66405.3	1151.11	2207.25
Lit	B	3546.90	19179.0	21813.0	73157.0	1959.84	–	64928.0	1084.10	2078.79
Netherlands	S	5.58700	30.2100	34.3600	115.2350	3.08700	1.5400	–	1.84050	3.52950
	C	5.46286	29.5389	33.5953	112.6730	3.01848	1.50590	–	1.73345	3.32389
Fl	B	5.34150	28.8825	32.8475	110.1675	2.95100	1.47250	–	1.63250	3.13050
Spain	S	334.619	1809.40	2057.80	6901.70	184.892	92.2400	6125.30	–	203.600
	C	315.143	1704.05	1938.06	6500.00	174.131	86.8726	5768.83	–	191.750
Pts	B	296.802	1604.90	1825.30	6121.70	163.997	81.8200	5433.10	–	180.590
United Kingdom	S	1.74510	9.43610	10.7320	35.9970	0.964240	0.481050	31.9450	0.553740	–
	C	1.64352	8.88687	10.1073	33.8984	0.908116	0.453053	30.0853	0.521514	–
£	B	1.54790	8.36970	9.5190	31.9280	0.855260	0.426690	28.3340	0.491160	–

S = Exchange rate at which the central bank of the country in the left-hand column will sell the currency identified in the row at the top of the table
C = Bilateral central rate.
B = Exchange rate at which the central bank of the country in the left-hand column will buy the currency identified in the row at the top of the table.

Source: Bank of England Quarterly Review
Table 14.2 ERM parity grid October 1990

As well as the individual central banks of member countries intervening, there was also established as part of the ERM a **European Monetary Co-operative Fund (EMCF)** into which member countries were forced to deposit 20% of their dollar and gold reserves.

Although some initial realignments of exchange rate values proved to be necessary in the first few years of the ERM, it quickly established itself as an effective means of reducing speculative pressure on currency and also dealing with domestic inflation.

When Britain eventually joined the ERM in 1990 it did so at a rate of DM2.95. This proved to be a fatal mistake. The markets believed that sterling was over-valued and would be unable to compete at DM2.95. At the same time pressures within Germany, such as the costs of reunification, caused the build-up of inflationary pressure, to which the Bundesbank responded by raising interest rates. As the DM rose in value against other member countries currencies, notably against the pound, sterling began to fall. Interest rates, which it was hoped would fall to stimulate domestic demand, were forced to remain high to retain confidence in sterling.

On what is now called **Black Wednesday**, 16th September 1992, almost two years following the UK's membership, sterling was withdrawn from the ERM. Even after extensive borrowing to protect the value of the pound (£7.25bn), and on Black Wednesday a 5% increase in interest rates, speculative pressure was not reduced and the pounds fate was sealed. On leaving the ERM the pound fell by almost 20% of its ERM value by October 1992.

Problems with the ERM did not end there. It's credibility as a means to manage exchange rates was seriously undermined by Black Wednesday, and it was not long before the speculators turned their attention to a new currency, namely the French franc. By late 1993 the ERM had in all but name been abandoned. Downward pressure on the franc and a reluctance by the Germans to relax interest rates forced the ERM to be revised and the bands around the agreed central rate to widen to + or − 15%.

As a key component of monetary union the failure of the ERM is a significant blow to this goal. It raises many issues not only concerning how to effectively manage exchange rates, but whether the nations that make up the EU will be able to deepen the relationship between them beyond merely a trade bloc.

Activity

The speed of change in the EU is such that new issues are appearing all of the time. Consulting recent quality newspapers and journals, discover what is being debated at present and assess its implications for the future course of European union by the year 2000.

Summary

The EU plays an influential part in shaping modern business practice and performance in all European economies. The creation of the SEA means that the national market is now Europe, geographical barriers are easily crossed and the removal of all internal trade restrictions for goods, labour and capital, mean that businesses must broaden their horizons and reassess their business strategy faced with such new opportunities.

Further reading

Livesey F, *Economics*, Longman, (1991) Chap 23 Section 23.4.

Hare P and Simpson L, *British Economic Policy*, Harvester Wheatsheaf, (1993), Chap 7.

Progress questions

1. The European Community was established in: ....

2. The four principal institutions of the EU are: ....

   ....

3. The most important source of revenue for the EU is VAT.   True ☐ False ☐

4. The final stage of monetary union would involve having a single central bank.

   True ☐ False ☐

5. The four criteria required for convergence are: ....

   ....

6. ERM stands for: ....

7. The ERM bands were $2\frac{1}{4}$ for all nations.   True ☐ False ☐

8. The day the UK left the ERM is known as RED MONDAY/BLACK WEDNESDAY.

Review questions

9. Why is regional policy so important for successful European union? (Section 14.3)

10. Explain how monetary union is to be achieved and consider the problems it is likely to encounter. (Section 14.3)

11. How does the ERM operate? (Section 14.4)

Multiple choice questions

12. The goal of European monetary union is to:
    (a) establish a single European market.
    (b) ensure that all member countries join the ERM.
    (c) introduce a single European currency.
    (d) All the above.

13. Which of the following institutions has most influence over the policy of the European Union.
    (a) The European Parliament.
    (b) The European Court of Justice.
    (c) The Council of Ministers.
    (d) The European Commission.

Practice questions

14. What advantages does the UK gain from being a member of the European Union?

15. Explain why the ERM collapsed and identify why semi-fixed exchange rates are difficult to maintain in the long run.

Assignment

In this assignment you are to set up a role play and debate the issue concerning the UK's future membership of the European Union. The following groups should be represented; politicians; business owners and mangers; and consumers. Each of these groups should be further split into those who wish the UK to remain in the union and those who do not. Good debating.

Answers to progress questions

Chapter 1

1. *False.* It is the study of aggregate consumer behaviour.
2. (i) *the firm*, (ii) *the market*, (iii) *the national economy*, (iv) *the international economy*.
3. A PEST analysis is *a consideration of political, economic, social and technological factors that influence a businesses performance and shape its business strategy.*

Chapter 2

1. *scarcity.*
2. *land, labour, capital* and *enterprise.*
3. The opportunity cost of a good is *the cost of one good in respect to another.*
4. the *planned economy, free market economy* and *mixed economy.*
5. *False.* A planned economy tends to offer a narrow range of consumer goods.
6. *False.* A free market economy tends to experience uncertainty due to fluctuations in supply and demand.
7. An externality is *a cost (or benefit) of production that is not included in the price of the product produced.*
8. Public goods are goods that the market will be unwilling to produce, whereas merit goods are goods that the market will fail to produce in sufficient quantity.
9. Three forms of state intervention might include *the direct provision of goods and services, economic policy and legal restrictions.*
10. Privatisation means *the return of state owned assets to the private sector*

Chapter 3

1. Three differences are *the number of owners, possibilities for expansion, a sole trader is personally liable for the business's loans.*
2. False. M-form management structures enable management to have a greater span of control.
3. *Profits, sales* and *growth.*
4. *True.*
5. Five reasons why growth is good for the economy are *higher investment, greater economies of scale, technological advances, productivity growth, better management.*
6. Internal expansion involves growth by ploughing back profits, issuing shares or borrowing. Growth by merger involves purchasing existing businesses to expand.
7. *Diversification, vertical integration and R & D.*
8. *True.*
9. *False.* Diseconomies of scale can only be removed in the long run.

10. Four reasons why big business might operate against the public interest are *the use of barriers to entry to restrict competition, charge higher prices, produce lower levels of output, suffer from inefficiency.*

Chapter 4

1. *inverse.*
2. *direct.*
3. Six factors might be *consumer tastes, the price of substitute goods, the price of complementary goods, the level of consumer income, advertising, future expectations.*
4. Four factors might be *the costs of production, producer aims, profitable alternative products, expectations of future price changes.*
5. A market equilibrium is when *demand equals supply.*
6. An elastic good is one that is *responsive to a change in a determinant such as price.*
7. An inelastic good is one that is *unresponsive to a change in a determinant such as price.*
8. *False.* Values of less than 1 signify an inelastic demand curve.
9. Cross price elasticity measures the responsiveness in demand for one good following a change in price of another good.
10. *False.* A negative elasticity value identifies an inferior good.

Chapter 5

1. The *short run* is where at least one factor of production is fixed in supply. In the *long run* all factors are variable.
2. *True.*
3. Total costs = fixed costs + variable costs
4. Average revenue equals price because it reflect the revenue earned from each unit of output.
5. *False.* When total revenue and total cost are furthest apart profits are maximised.
6. Where MC=MR the business will know the point of profit maximisation.
7. Three reasons are; a problem of information, profit maximisation might not be a business goal, prices are set in response to changes in the market.
8. Three alternative pricing strategy are; incremental pricing, mark-up pricing, breakeven pricing.
9. *False.* Market skimming involves going in with a high price to skim of profits.
10. Three factors are; business strategy, retail economies of scale, consumer lifestyle.

Chapter 6

1. The four main market structures are: perfect competition, monopoly, monopolistic competition and oligopoly.
2. *False.* In perfect competition businesses are price takers.
3. *True.*
4. Supernormal profits are those above that would keep the business in the market.
5. *True.*
6. Three advantages are: efficiency, economies of scale and supernormal profits enable new products to be developed.
7. *True.*

8. *True.*

9. Six factors that might favour collusion are: fewer businesses, no secrecy, similar production costs, threats of new competition, market stability and government attitudes towards collusion.

10. A barometric price leader is a business that responds well to market changes and is thus followed by other businesses.

Chapter 7

1. Three criteria might be market share, ownership or level of employment.

2. *True.*

3. *False.* Small businesses find it difficult to raise finance.

4. Three forms of assistance might include: business start-up schemes, policies to help firms grow and policies to improve economic performance.

5. A multinational company might be defined as a company that owns or controls production or service facilities outside the country in which it is based.

6. *True.*

7. Multinational investment might be encouraged because it creates employment. (Other factors might have included investment, technology or a contribution to the balance of payments).

8. Five reasons might include: the level of competition, the repatriation of profits, uncertainty, the loss of control over business, the use of the environment, e.g. natural resource depletion.

Chapter 8

1. The rise in service sector employment and the decline in industrial employment.

2. *A movement along* the labour supply curve.

3. The MRP_L refers to the additional revenue earned per additional worker.

4. *Diminishing returns.*

5. Collective bargaining is the title given to the process of negotiation between employers and employees.

6. Six factors might include; union power; the level of profits; productivity; the cost of living; the comparability of wage settlements; the state of the economy.

7. *Fall.*

8. Five ways in which legislation has changed working practices are; unions can face legal action for unlawful industrial action; secondary picketing is illegal; strikes must be conducted by secret ballot; union leaders must seek regular re-election; wages councils have been abolished.

9. Japanese working practices involve; TQM; JIT; team working and flexibility.

10. *True.*

Chapter 9

1. Investment can be defined as the process of adding to the stock of capital assets.

2. *True.*

3. Five factors that will influence investment are; the rate of interest; current profits; expectations of the future; costs and productivity of capital; access to finance.

4. An investment projects cash flow is the flow of profits over the projects lifetime.

5. *True.*

6. The rate of discount is the rate at which we convert expected future cash flows back to present values.

7. Three forms of investment finance are; share issues; borrowing; profits.

8. *False.* The gearing ratio is the ratio of debt to equity finance.

9. *True.*

10 Four ways that training and economic performance are linked are; workers with relevant skills; quantity of skilled labour; quality of skills held by workforce; multi-skilled workers are more flexible.

Chapter 10

1. *True.*

2. *True.* Please note that the availability of other resources would also be important.

3. GDP measures national wealth.

4. Aggregate demand consists of consumption, investment, government expenditure and earnings from exports.

5. The trade cycle shows the cyclical performance of the economy.

6. *True.*

7. *True.*

8. The multiplier can be defined as the multiplied effect upon the level of economic activity from a given change in the level of aggregate demand.

9. *Inflationary*

10. *Expectations*

Chapter 11

1. Four functions of money are; as a medium of exchange; a means of storing value; a unit of account; a standard of deferred payment.

2. *False.* Money might include any form of payment that is readily convertible to cash, such as cheques.

3. *True.*

4. *MO* and *M4*.

5. Five functions of the Bank of England might include: the issuing of notes and coin; banker to government; banker to the banks; managing the national debt; managing foreign currency reserves.

6. *True.*

7. *False.* A discount house is a financial intermediary that deals in short term lending to the commercial banks and sells government securities to the market.

8. *Money market* and *capital market*.

9. The liquidity ratio is the ratio of liquid to illiquid assets.

10. Inflation can be defined as the given change in prices over a particular period, such as a year.

Chapter 12

1. The four principle objectives of government are; low unemployment, high growth; low inflation; a favourable balance of payments.

2. *True.*

3. *True.*

4. Demand side policy focus upon consumer demand and income.

5. Fiscal stance refers to the expansionary or contractionary position of the governments budget.

6. *True.*

7. *Sell.*

8. *Buy.*

9. Five forms of free market supply side policy are; privatisation; reductions in government expenditure; reduced rates of personal taxation; the removal of union rights; the reduction in welfare benefits.

10. *True.*

Chapter 13

1. The terms of trade refer to the quantity of imports gained from a given quantity of exports.

2. *True.*

3. *True.*

4. Two advantages of a high pound are; low import prices, and business is forced to become more cost competitive and hence efficient.

5. *Fall.*

6. *Depreciation.*

7. Three forms of long term intervention are; direct controls on goods and services; expenditure changing policy; and devaluation or revaluation of the exchange rate.

8. *True.*

9. Three arguments against protectionism are; retaliation; ill-will; inefficient producers.

10. Three organizations that have improved international policy co-operation are the World Bank, the IMF, and the GATT.

Chapter 14

1. 1958.

2. The four principle institutions are; the European Parliament; the European Commission; the Council of Ministers; the European Court of Justice.

3. *True.*

4. *True.*

5. The four convergence criteria are; a stable exchange rate; price stability; a stable level of government spending; stable interest rates.

6. ERM stands for Exchange Rate Mechanism.

7. *False.* The UK and Spain had bands of 6%.

8. *Black Wednesday.*

Index

Tackling Coursework
Projects, Assignments, Reports and Presentations

David Parker

This book provides the student with practical guidance on how to approach the course-work requirement of a typical business studies course, i.e. projects, assignments, reports and presentations. The text makes clear the different approaches needed for the different types of coursework, with examples of each in an Appendix, and there is advice on how to conduct research, collect information and present results, in either written or verbal form. It is expected to be used on the following courses: any business studies course at undergraduate (e.g. BABS) or postgraduate (e.g. MBA) level. It would also be useful as a preparatory text for a research degree.

Contents

Introduction, Dissertations and projects, Essays and papers, Management reports, Seminars and presentations, Research methods. **Appendices:** *Further reading, Example of a dissertation proposal, Example of citations, Dissertation contents, Example of an essay.*

1st edition • 96 pp • 215 x 135 mm • 1994 • ISBN 1 85805 101 0